WORDS OF PRAISE FOR
"MOM, CAN I PLAY FOOTBALL?"

"As a coach, Jerry Norton had a great influence on my children. He has written an intelligent, witty and reflective book demonstrating that it is, indeed, possible for children to develop their natural abilities, learn good sportsmanship and also have fun playing youth sports.
A *"Should Read"* for coaches. A *"Must Read"* for parents."
— Dr. J. Gerald Meagher, **MD. F.A.C.S.**
Obstetrics and Gynecology, Huntington, NY

"The job of a great youth coach is to provide the same wonderful experience for all participants, both the talented and the less talented. Jerry Norton does just that. *Mom, Can I Play Football?* is a giant step forward for youth sports. It is the blueprint for making sports enjoyable for all children."
— Corey Miller, **Former player, UVA Alumnus,**
New York, NY

"I thoroughly enjoyed reading *Mom Can I Play Football?* What a valuable resource it will become for young football players and their families, especially the mothers."
— Lisa A. March, Esquire, **Mother of two young**
football players, Ponte Vedra Beach, FL

"The simplicity of the book's message and the illustrations make it a delight to read. Anyone who has ever played sports or coached kids will enjoy it. Anyone intending to coach children should be required to read it."
— Joseph Bowers, **Former major college and high**
school football coach, Ponte Vedra Beach, FL

"As a sports marketing professional and sports mom, I think this book should be required reading for all coaches and sports parents. Don't enter youth sports without it!"
— Colleen Clarson, **Owner, Sport Concepts,**
Ponte Vedra Beach, FL

MOM, CAN I PLAY
FOOTBALL?

An Introspective View of the
Game for Parents and Coaches

BY JERRY NORTON

SIDELINE PRESS
Ponte Vedra Beach, FL

Sideline Press
105 Old Ponte Vedra Dr.
Ponte Vedra Beach, FL 32082 USA

First printing August 1999

10   9   8   7   6   5   4   3   2   1

Manufactured in the United States of America

Cover and Interior Design by Lightbourne

Library of Congress Catalog Card Number: 99-95087

ISBN: 0-9673456-0-X

CONTENTS

ACKNOWLEDGMENTS

Far too many people contributed to this book, either directly or indirectly, for me to acknowledge each of them separately. To this entire group, let me say I am grateful to you all.

More specifically, my wife, Marylou, and my children, Scott, David and Chris, encouraged me to start this project, provided honest criticism and helped enormously with specifics when my memory let me down.

Cindy Richetti, a friend and a fantastic sports mom, helped with editing and made many valuable suggestions.

Over the past 35 years, I met many excellent youth coaches and much of what I learned from them along the way is reflected in this book. So also is what I learned from the overzealous coaches I encountered. I thank both groups for their inspiration.

All of the children I had the privilege of coaching (and their parents) certainly had a profound influence on me and, hence, on this book. Thank you all for the pleasure of your company.

Thanks to Chester Villar, whose delightful illustrations make the book so enjoyable and easy to read.

Thanks to Gaelyn Larrick, Shannon Bodie and Paula Martin of Lightbourne for their sage advice and for turning my manuscript into this handsome book.

Thanks to Houghton Mifflin and Dr. Lyle Micheli, author of *Sportswise: An Essential Guide for Young Athletes, Coaches and Parents* for granting me permission to quote from his book concerning injury rates in Pop Warner football.

Thanks also to the National Alliance for Youth Sports for allowing me to reprint their Standards For Developing and Administering Youth Sports Programs, their Code of Conduct for Coaches and their Code of Ethics for Parents. I was delighted to learn about this vital organization just before going to press and to find that we share a common philosophy regarding youth sports. Their brief mission statement best describes this philosophy:

Better Sports For Kids—Better Kids For Life.

Dedication

To my three sons, Scott, David and Chris,
for getting me involved so many years ago,
and
To all the wonderful children I have met
and
To all of wonderful children I have yet to meet
as a result.

"MOM, CAN I PLAY FOOTBALL?"

THE PREGAME WARM-UP

WHY THIS BOOK?

I f you have, or will soon have little children, some time, some day, probably when you are least prepared, you will face one of life's really critical decisions. It will happen the day your young child sidles up to you and asks out of a clear blue sky, "Mom, can I play football?" Your response could have major repercussions on family peace and tranquillity for years to come, and you should therefore consider the request quite seriously.

Now, it is likely you and your spouse have not spent three seconds discussing this matter, since your little person never mentioned football even once before.

Some possible responses to this innocent child's question might flash through your mind— "absolutely no," "forget it," "don't even think about it," "are you crazy," "when pigs can fly," "of course not, you're a girl," "maybe next year," "I'll think about it," "go ask your father" or possibly even "certainly, my dear"—any of which might seem appropriate. But there is sure to be some subsequent and possibly heated discussion of the matter between you and the player candidate or your parental partner.

Will you be prepared to respond convincingly,

2 · MOM, CAN I PLAY FOOTBALL?

pro or con? Or do you feel the need for some Solomon-like guidance or expert counsel to deal with this controversial situation?

Mom, Can I Play Football? is intended to help you through this difficult time, perhaps make you feel better about your decision—or maybe even reconsider an unfavorable decision. If you're a dad who would like to get involved as a coach, but you're not sure how to go about it, this book can really help.

If none of the above situations applies, but you're interested in kids sports or intrigued by the title— please read on. This book is not a technical manual about coaching football, full of Xs and Os, diagramming my favorite plays, although it *is* intended to educate parents, grandparents, coaches and prospective coaches of young football players. It's really about little kids—how to coach them, what to expect and what not to expect from them, and some of the funny and wonderful things they do. These lessons emerge from my 30-plus years of coaching children.

Youth football can be an exciting and very memorable experience for young children and their parents. All that is necessary is the right situation. That means the right type of program, with good coaches and the right equipment. *Mom, Can I Play Football?* considers these three important ingredients in the context of today's environment.

THE NAME OF THE GAME IS FUN

While the focus of this book is on youth football, much of what it discussed in the following chapters is appropriate for any sport. Indeed, my guiding philosophy concerning sports and children is independent of the ball used or the game played. This philosophy is quite simple. First, sports should be fun for kids. Second, it is the coaches' job to make and keep the sport fun. And third, for kids to have fun, they must play, not sit on the bench.

Things change, of course, as players grow up. Although the fun aspect remains to some degree, scholastic, collegiate and professional competitive sports focus less on fun and more on winning. In the extreme, in professional sports, fun is no longer a consideration. The coach is responsible for winning, not for making the sport fun, and only the best players are given an opportunity to play. Keeping this ever-increasing focus on winning from happening too soon in a child's athletic life is the youth coach's foremost and most daunting responsibility. Explaining to coaches and parents how this can be accomplished is really my ultimate objective.

DO YOU MEASURE UP?

Step away from football for a moment and consider that the important ingredients in any sports program for children are fun and participation. With this thought in mind, take this short parents' quiz to find out about your potential as a good sport parent and learn how this book can benefit you and your child.

Parents' Quiz

1. Can you tell the difference between a soccer ball and a football?

☐ Yes   ☐ No

2. Has your child ever indicated a desire to play competitive kids sports?

☐ Yes   ☐ No

3. Have you ever wondered what goes on at a kids sports practice? (baseball, football, soccer, etc.)

☐ Yes   ☐ No

4. Do you wish you could spend more time having fun with your children?

☐ Yes   ☐ No

5. Did you have a pleasant experience playing sports as a child?

☐ Yes   ☐ No

6. Is patience one of your virtues?

☐ Yes   ☐ No

If you responded yes to all six questions you are, more than likely, a willing and eager youth sport parent. If you are not yet involved in kids' sports, finish reading this book, then run out and sign your child up in a sports program and volunteer your services. Youth programs always need parents like you. You and your child will have a wonderful time simply by following the conceptual suggestions offered on these pages. If your child is already involved, use the information in this book to judge your own involvement, the program and the coaches, and initiate improvements if necessary.

If you answered yes to a majority of these questions, talk to your child about participating, and investigate programs available in your community. This book will help you choose a good program, and if you are interested in coaching, it will give you specific suggestions on how to keep games fun and exciting. With a little encouragement you can discover an opportunity you'll both enjoy. If your child is already into sports, this book will help you evaluate the quality of the program and its coaches and give you the support to change things if need be.

If you made just one or two yes responses, your involvement in youth sports may just be as an occasional spectator. If so, this book will help you to understand and maintain a healthy and wholesome perspective as a fan and a parent. Again, this book will help you evaluate or improve your child's program.

Finally, if you have children and failed to make any yes responses, you may want to reconsider the priorities in your life. This book will help you understand the fun you both are missing.

"HI, MOM!"

HENCE THE TITLE

Now let's get back to my favorite subject, football. While I was trying to decide on a title for this book, I was reminded of how football players, when captured on TV after making a big play, invariably wave into the camera and shout, "Hi, Mom!" Dad may have been their first coach, their most vocal critic and their most loyal fan, but mom's the one they wave and say hi to.

It might be that football players always acknowledge mom because they understand that mom worries about them, and they want to let her know they are okay. Many moms are not eager to have their children play football in the first place. They are concerned about the dangers and the risk of injury. Most moms never played football themselves and therefore may not have that special feeling about the game that dads, who did play, may have. Whatever the reason, mom is usually the parent who needs to be convinced if a child is to play football, and since I'm in favor of kids playing the game, it seems appropriate to make my case to mom through her child; hence the title.

Do I hope to change the world with this writing? No, at least not all of it. Perhaps just that small part occupied by little kids with a ball and their coach.

ABOUT THE AUTHOR

Before going any further, let me tell you a bit about myself and my experience with the subject of kids and football. I am the father of three sons, Scott, David and Chris, who grew up in the 1960s and 70s and who were typical of their generation. They belonged to the Cub Scouts and Boy Scouts, took piano lessons and played the organized youth sport of the season. As an encouraging parent and eager volunteer, I took great pleasure in participating in their leisure activities, serving faithfully for years as coach and as scout leader.

I coached my boys' baseball and football teams for nearly a decade, until they moved on to high school. It was so enjoyable, I continued to coach football, baseball and girls' softball and served as an officer in our church youth program long after my children grew up.

I retired happily from my job as an electronics engineer in 1992, after 40 years with the Grumman Aerospace Corporation and now spend much of my time covering youth sports for our local weekly newspaper. Sports writing is not a job but a passion. It's all about kids and it's fun. I'm still coaching football and currently have an 8-year-old Pop Warner team. Will I ever retire from coaching? Probably not, it's too much fun.

My formative years were spent in Kenmore, NY, a suburb of Buffalo, in the early 1940s. Little league baseball and organized midget football leagues were practically non-existent back then. Those that did exist were few and far between. Kenmore must have been somewhere "in between".

As kids, we didn't let the lack of organized leagues stand in our way for a minute. We played sports all the time. I'd say I was a jock before I even knew what a jock was—not a good one, mind you, but a jock nonetheless. Some time between the ages of 8 and 12, I must have played almost every sport known to man, certainly all of the big ones . . . baseball, football, basketball, hockey, tennis, even wrestling.

Our activities were never organized in any sense of the word . . . just a group of kids in a field somewhere having fun. Of course there wasn't a parent within miles. Equipment was practically non-existent, except for the absolute necessities like a football, a baseball wrapped with black "friction tape," a wooden bat wrapped in the same black tape, a racket of sorts, or skates. None of us who played hockey, for example, had real shin guards. Instead, we wrapped copies of *Life* magazine around our legs and held them in place with rubber bands cut from old automobile inner tubes. We made do, or we did without. Equipment just wasn't very important back then. Playing was.

Pro football was in its infancy. College football was king, and high school football was also very big in Buffalo. During the war years, the service academies had a lock on many of the good athletes, so Army and Navy both fielded some of their best teams ever.

Because my dad was an old Navy man, I was a serious midshipmen fan. At that time, the Naval Academy had a halfback by the name of Clyde

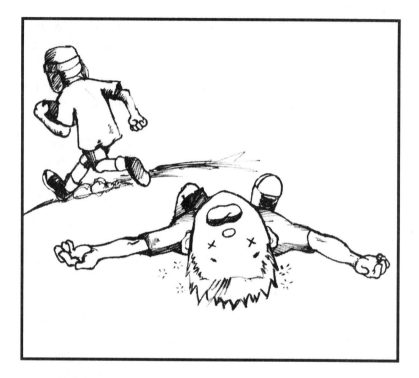

"BEFORE HELMETS WERE REQUIRED"

"Smackover" Scott. Isn't that a great name for a football player? Smackover!! It was said that he got the nickname from his home town of Smackover, Arkansas. He was my favorite player. A picture of him with a straight arm up, one knee high and the ball tucked under his arm, sort of like the Heisman trophy pose, hung over my bed.

Scott's first name, Clyde, was my dad's name and my brother's name so it was as if he were one of the family. Unfortunately for Navy, Army had two guys named "Mr. Inside" and "Mr. Outside"—Felix "Doc" Blanchard and Glenn Davis. These two were as good as any pair of backs who ever played football, so Army usually won the big inter-service game in those days.

As you might have guessed by now, football was and still is my very favorite sport. Every Saturday morning in the fall (except for one notable Saturday you will hear about later), I would grab my old hand-me-down football pants—the disgusting orange-brown color of that day—that had long ago lost their thigh pad inserts, and my skimpy red cardboard shoulder pads, and head for the nearby school field where we would play tackle with reckless abandon for hours on end. There were no goalposts and no lines on the field, no first-down chains and no yard markers. We took turns playing offense and defense. No one ever won or lost.

There were no playbooks nor any deceptive plays, for that matter, because everyone always knew who was going to carry the ball . . . it would be the guy wearing the helmet. You see, only one kid in our group had a helmet, and the ball carrier wore it.

Soon, we would all get a chance to play on a real

"PLEEEASE, MOM. IT'S A
GREEN-AND-WHITE GAME!"

team, or so we thought. One particular Saturday a new group of kids showed up at the field all wearing green-and-white jerseys. Quite a few of them also wore helmets. It was rumored that they were rich kids from the other side of town.

One of the kids, a short rusty-haired boy named Tommy, came up and asked if we would like to play them in a real game. We agreed instantly. We got "stomped on," big time. But after the game, Tommy invited us all to play on his team. He said he would arrange games against some other street teams. This was just about as good as it could possibly get. A real team with a real captain playing real games. We might even get real uniforms. A dream come true!

Our group continued to meet every Saturday and play with, or to be more precise, against, the "Green and Whites." No other teams ever showed up. For that matter, none of my team ever got a green-and-white jersey either. But that was okay; we now had more guys and we were still playing football.

As mentioned earlier, we played football every Saturday in the fall, except for this one Saturday. I had gotten up early as usual and was heading out the door with my "stuff" when my Mom stopped me, saying, "Not so fast, young man." I knew I was in for trouble; she called me "young man." "You are not going anywhere today; you are going to stay home and clean the garage." I was devastated. "Please, Mom, it's a 'Green and White' game!" I wailed. But no amount of tears or pleading would change her mind. I had to clean the garage.

It was clearly the worst day of my short life. It helped only slightly that the Army-Navy game was broadcast on radio that day. But even that turned out wrong—Navy lost again. To this day, cleaning the garage is my least favorite chore.

It wasn't long before real organized football became available. It was in junior high school with real coaches, real opponents, real uniforms and real equipment. Everyone got their own helmet. True, they didn't have face masks, but who knew about face masks in those days?

My first year in "organized football" was, like the remainder of my football career, utterly undistinguished but totally and thoroughly enjoyable. It probably didn't mean anything then, but it stands in sharp contrast to today to note that neither of my parents ever watched me play a single down in any game.

Except for one brief season of semi-pro ball on Long Island after I was married, my playing career ended. I enjoyed every minute of it, even though I have to admit I was just an average player, at best.

So many of my cherished childhood memories are centered around this game we played as youngsters. Wonderful recollections occupy a special place in my mind, retrievable on demand. Sometimes they even flood out without request, triggered by a crisp autumn day—the smell of burning leaves or a bonfire—driving past a high school football practice—the mere mention of an upcoming Army-Navy game—or the utterance of a single word . . . "football." I can't imagine what I would be like today if I had not had these experiences.

Nor am I the least embarrassed or ashamed to

2ly22ly ready!222222

admit there is little that excites me more these days than being around young kids playing football. Even after so many years, each new season brings new excitement, new situations, new lessons and, most importantly, new players eager to play and enjoy the game. I'm only sorry I didn't take good notes along the way. I'd have enough hilarious anecdotes, wonderfully humorous examples and important lessons for coaches and parents to fill several books. It is from these experiences, memories and lessons that this book emerges.

Are you ready for some football? I'm always ready!

"YESTERDAY AND TODAY"

YESTERDAY'S EXPERIENCE
VS. TODAY'S GAME

There is little similarity between the football we played as youngsters and organized youth football that kids now play. Today, players must be safely equipped, they have regular practices with supervised instruction and play regularly scheduled games on lined and manicured fields with goalposts and teams of adult referees in black-and-white-striped uniforms. Parents fill up the stands and cheer wildly for their team, usually at the urging of a bevy of brightly uniformed cheerleaders with multi-colored pom-poms.

Some adults argue that the old spontaneous sandlot pick-up game of the past, without equipment, coaches, referees, parents and hoopla, is preferred over today's highly structured and organized event. It is not my intention to join in this debate. We enjoyed our game, and kids today can and should enjoy their game—if it is done right. What does it take to do it right? Read on.

Experts are also debating whether participating in sports develops character, prepares a child for adult life or promotes a child's social development. This deep and philosophical exercise is better left to the trained and educated professional.

Regardless of the conclusions that may someday be reached, organized youth sports are a reality today. Millions of children between the ages of 4 and 14 are participating, and nearly as many adults are coaching. Parents and coaches need to do everything possible to make sure these programs are safe, enjoyable and beneficial.

THE COIN TOSS

TO PLAY OR NOT TO PLAY?

Today's parents are often reluctant to allow their children to play football. In my day, permission was never an issue; kids just went out and played. The reasons parents give for not allowing their child to play these days are numerous and varied including "he might get hurt," "he's too small," "she's a girl," "we'll wait until high school," and "the coaches are crazy." Let's examine each of these issues.

"It's Too Dangerous. He Might Get Hurt. We'll Wait Until High School."

Many parents think football is too dangerous. More than likely, these feelings come from watching high school, college or NFL games and seeing or hearing about catastrophic injuries. Certainly televising of NFL games provides supporting evidence for this position. Monday Night Football is very popular, but it is definitely not an endorsement for youth football. The differences between professional, college and even high school football and a properly run youth football program are dramatic and become even greater the younger the player.

A properly run youth football program considers the size and age of the participants. Players are usually grouped according to both age and weight. Special rules, designed to simplify the game and minimize injury or avoid potentially dangerous situations, usually exist at the younger age groups.

In the lighter weight and younger age divisions of a youth program, the players simply do not run as fast, weigh as much or hit as hard as players who are older, bigger and stronger. The proper equipment plus good coaching of proper blocking and tackling techniques further minimizes the risk of injury. The result is that youth football can be quite safe.

In *Sportswise: An Essential Guide for Young Athletes, Parents and Coaches*, Dr. Lyle Micheli, doctor of sports medicine and past president of the American College of Sports Medicine states, " . . . in Pop Warner football, which is for children below the age of fourteen, injuries are very rare because the quality of supervision is very high."

Dr. Micheli goes on to say, "On the other hand, soccer, which has a reputation for being a safe sport for both sexes, has been shown to have a high injury rate, particularly among the younger children."

My own experience is that equipment, safety awareness and injury prevention have improved dramatically to the point that injuries to young football players are indeed rare, especially so at the youngest ages.

So what about the parent who says, "I don't want my eight-year-old to play football because he might get hurt. I think we'll wait until he goes to high school to let him play." There are two problems with this line of reasoning. The most obvious is that the risk of injury for the 8-year-old is slight while the risk of injury as a high school player is significantly higher.

Second, the youngster who waits until high school to play football is at a distinct disadvantage compared to his classmates who may have been playing for several years. The player may have difficulty making the high school team, and if he doesn't, he will have missed out on a wonderful experience. It really doesn't make any sense to me. Kids should start playing when they are young if they wish to do so.

"But She's A Girl."

"Times, they are a changin'." Federal and state laws require schools to provide equal access to sports for boys and girls. As a result, an increasing number of girls are enjoying traditionally male sports both in high school and in the lower-age youth programs. Today, many youth baseball and soccer programs are coed, and girls are also finding their way onto Pop Warner football rosters. There are even some girls' football leagues at the high school level.

Three young girls played in our local football program recently—an 8-year-old and two 10-year-olds. The girls all said they played because they thought it would be fun and wanted to experience the traditional boys' game.

According to medical experts, both boys and girls who have developed strength, flexibility and conditioning can play football safely. A pre-sports physical for both sexes including a "sports-specific" fitness level is recommended.

If your daughter has a desire to play football and is physically qualified, a well-run youth program for 8- or 9-year-olds could be the perfect answer. It may be her only opportunity to experience and enjoy the

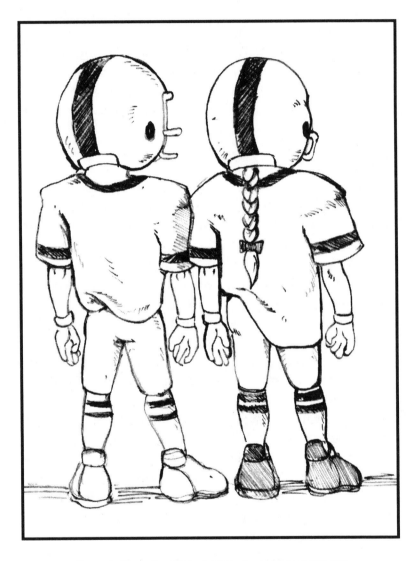

"TIMES THEY ARE A CHANGIN'"

game. Just think of the greater appreciation of the game she will enjoy for a lifetime, even if she discontinues her involvement later.

"The Coaches Are Crazy."

You may believe, by now, that concerns about safety in youth football are not supported by the evidence. Unfortunately, complaints about overzealous coaches are too often justified. There are such coaches at the youth level, as well as at higher levels. You've heard about them, the ones who will do anything to win. Who treat their players like animals, not little children. Who think they are the second coming of Vince Lombardi and who think every game is the Super Bowl. Mostly they are adults with big egos and little concern for kids.

It doesn't have to be this way, though. Something can be done about it. It is possible for good coaches to drive the bad ones to the sidelines and on into extinction. What it will take is for you, potentially a good coach, to get involved. Of course, you will need to understand how to be a good coach, but that is the easy part. You're reading this book, so you're probably almost there. Subsequent chapters will help you. The hardest part is to make the time and then go out and do it.

Having disposed of the more common negatives, let's now consider some of the positive aspects of youth football. First, football is so much more than a game with a final score. It is a game within a game in which each player competes on every play with the player opposite him. If the offensive player's block is

"THE DICTATOR"

effective, the play may be successful. It may even result in a touchdown. If the defensive player sheds the block and makes a tackle, the defense is successful, and a touchdown is denied. If the offensive player's block is less than perfect, most observers aren't aware of it, the player is not embarrassed and, just as important, gets another chance to succeed on the very next play. Even if the team doesn't win, the players can feel good about their overall performance. It's a wonderful way for kids to compete.

Football is a fun game and a very popular sport for all ages with local teams and local heroes. Both girls and boys dream and fantasize about playing football. Youth programs can provide a safe opportunity to play and learn. The game is exciting with continuous action and individual competition on every play. The player's next opportunity is just seconds away.

Football can enhance a player's self-esteem, physical dexterity and fitness. Players learn and understand the need for discipline, teamwork and individual responsibility. Success and accomplishment are within reach of all players with little pressure. The necessary skills are easily mastered.

Football is a team sport where the team's success is the result of contributions by all players, not just a few individuals. This shared responsibility for winning or losing makes the outcome of the game easier for young kids to handle. Failures by individuals are not apparent for all to see.

Finally, youth football provides a strong foundation for individuals who will play later in high school and gives these players an advantage over candidates who have not played before.

"THREE STRIKES . . . YOU'RE OUT!"

BASEBALL OR FOOTBALL?

Don't get me wrong, I like baseball. I liked to play it, coach it and watch it. Each of my boys played baseball. It's the National Pastime. Many of my most precious memories of kids and sports come from little kids playing baseball.

Many experts think youngsters should try a variety of athletic activities in the course of growing up. If they play or focus on only one, they are missing out on a great deal of variety, fun and excitement. Concentrating on a single sport as a child can also lead to overemphasis and early burnout. Children should have the opportunity to try different sports to find the ones that suit their needs, their physical makeup and their temperament.

I totally agree and football should be one of the sports kids try. I encourage youngsters to try it every chance I get. Why? For all the good reasons listed previously, but mostly because it is fun. It really is what kids like to do most—roughhousing, rolling on the ground and getting dirty (without reprimand), running around and competing at a fast pace. Whether it's today's highly organized variety or my 1940s sandlot version, both have the basic elements of what is fun for kids—and isn't having fun the main reason kids play any game?

Kids also like to learn and master new skills, but are put off by extended frustration and stressful or embarrassing situations. A boy may give up trying to learn how to hit a baseball before he reaches a level of competence as a batter. In the process, his failures are visible to all.

"THERE"S A POSITION IN
FOOTBALL FOR EVERY BODY!"

The skills needed to play and succeed in football are not difficult to learn or to teach and do not require exceptional athleticism or years of patience and practice to master. While it is true that not everyone will excel at one of the more difficult positions like quarterback, there are seven other position categories requiring a range of physical attributes to accommodate varying player sizes, skills and abilities. The slower heavy child can become an outstanding center or defensive lineman. The tiny but fast little person can become a fine defensive back or running back.

A wise and successful youth football coach said it best: "Not everyone can do everything, but everyone can do something," and there is something in football for everyone and every *body*.

Given all of that, it is not surprising that football was the most popular boys' high school sport according to the National Federation of High School Associations in 1995. Football has always been my favorite, as a player, a spectator and a coach. But over the years as youth football moved from sandlot to organized, I've seen enough wacky coaches and overzealous adult fans to be concerned that young players or their sane and rational parents might be turned off by the game. Again, it doesn't have to be that way, which is part of the reason for this book.

"HAPPINESS IS A LITTLE GUY
MAKING A TACKLE"

THE PRACTICE EXPERIENCE

Football is quite different from almost any organized game kids play today. It has the basic ingredients of fun that turns kids on . . . rough and tumble, down and dirty, keen and continuous competition. And they can compete without the stigma of highly visible failure.

One of the biggest and perhaps the most important difference between football and most other sports is "the practice experience." Practice is an enormous part of a youngster's football experience and enjoyment. It consumes much more time than the player's game experience. Youth football teams typically practice four or five hours per week and play but a fraction of that in Saturday's game.

Football practice is controlled, usually quite intense and varied, with many opportunities for positive feedback for all the players. Because an individual player participates longer at practice than in a game, there are many more situations or opportunities for a youngster to make a successful, exciting or memorable play. It's important to remember that, in the young player's mind, a big play made in practice is no less a big play. Just look at the expression of joy on the face of the little quarterback who completes a pass for a touchdown in practice. Watch the reaction of the players when a little linebacker makes a big hit on the ball carrier in a tackling drill. That it didn't occur during a game is totally irrelevant.

Scrimmage time during football practice is very much like the game situation, and in some ways, it is even better than the game. The players play football and have fun. There are no penalties and no pressure and they don't have to deal with losing.

Because match-ups in practice are controlled, the coach can further enhance the less skilled player's opportunity to succeed by arranging a more equitable player pairing. For example, the coach can match a little player against another little player, thus ensuring the potential for a positive experience for both. Good coaches will use practice situations to promote a player's confidence and self-image. In addition, these frequent, positive, practice experiences go a long way to offset the momentary disappointment of a Saturday loss.

A FINAL WORD ON SAFETY

The catastrophic injury rate in football has declined markedly in the past 40 years for several important reasons. In the late 1960s the National Operating Committee on Standards in Athletic Equipment (NOCSAE) was created to develop standards of safety for athletic equipment. First on the committee's agenda was head protection for football players, and within a few years, a standard had been developed. By 1980, the National Collegiate Athletic Association and the National Federation of State High School Associations adopted the NOCSAE standard. Today all college, high school and organized youth players must wear a NOCSAE-certified helmet.

Rules have been changed prohibiting players from making initial contact with the helmet or face mask when blocking and tackling, and coaches at all levels are teaching the proper techniques. Clinics are held to ensure proper fit of the helmet and other equipment. Mouth pieces must be worn by all players. There is an increased emphasis on proper conditioning of players. At the younger levels of play, higher-risk situations, such as punts or kick-offs, are often prohibited or controlled. Advances such as these have been championed or embraced by reputable national youth football programs such as Pop Warner football, as well as many local organizations, which is why youth football injuries today are rare.

THE GAME

THE PROGRAM PRIORITIES

Very simply stated, the priorities for a good, wholesome youth sports program should be, in this order:

Priority Number 1—Safety

Priority Number 2—Fun

Priority Number 3—Learning/Development

These priorities must also be the individual coach's priorities. If they are not, players can suffer.

Quite obviously, the program and its coaches must put the players' safety above all else. The right kind of equipment, properly fitted, goes a long way in making a youth football program safe, but safety also requires that all coaches understand and follow safety procedures and precautions and teach safe blocking and tackling techniques. Organizations should provide special clinics and workshops to train their coaches in these safe playing techniques as well as basic first aid, CPR and methods of recognizing and avoiding injuries. The organization should have a medical emergency plan in place to deal with urgent medical situations at games and at practices. This plan must be understood by all coaches. Each team should have its own well-stocked medical kit to handle the inevitable bumps and bruises that occur.

After safety comes fun. To have fun kids must

"WAKE ME WHEN IT'S OVER!"

play, not sit on the bench during games or stand around at practice. Kids are, or should be, at least, participating for recreation and enjoyment. It is hoped that they will also learn how to play the game. It should not be the other way around, however, where learning is accomplished at the expense of fun and enjoyment. It is wrong for overzealous or abusive coaches to punish players who do not perform up to expectations (which are probably unrealistic). A player's punishment is typically in the form of extra pushups, extra laps or worse, isolation or banishment from further participation.

The less skilled players may have more difficulty performing in drills and often require extra attention. But the overzealous coach focuses on his better players and does not provide the lesser ones the instruction they need. As a result, practice for these kids is no longer fun, they are turned off and will probably quit before too long.

That of course doesn't bother the overzealous coach one bit. The coach simply brushes the situation off with, "That kid wasn't a football player anyway," and now there is one less substitute to squeeze into the game for the minimum number of plays on Saturday. The better players receive more playing time, thus improving the coach's chances of winning. *If a few more weaker players quit, we'd be even better off,* the coach may think.

Some degree of discipline is essential for most learning situations, and learning is certainly an important objective in youth football. It is a fine line that coaches must walk to instill discipline. They need to maintain discipline yet, at the same time, preserve player interest and enthusiasm. If the coach is too focused on winning, discipline and punishment overcome fun.

Instead of focusing on winning, the coach should concentrate on creative and exciting ways to keep all players enthusiastic and to inspire each of them to perform a little better at every practice. When the coach is doing the right things for all his players, progress and improvement become criteria for success, and winning is less likely to be overemphasized. Furthermore, the team's chances of winning are very likely to be enhanced by this approach.

It is should be clear by now that the coach sets the tone for almost everything that happens on the field. The coach also sets the tone for the behavior of fans in the stands. If the coach is under control and is having fun, the players and the fans are more likely to be under control and having a good time. If the coach is acting like a wild person, constantly yelling at the players, complaining about the other team or berating the game officials, chances are greater that his players and supporting fans will behave the same way. This behavior is typical of a coach consumed with the desire to win.

It was not an oversight that I did not include winning in my list of priorities. Coaches should coach to win, but should not let their desire to win take precedence over any player's safety, development or enjoyment of the game. The players must be encouraged to work hard to improve their skills and to always do their best. Kids try very hard to win, as they should. Certainly, they are happier if they do win. But surveys have shown most kids would rather *play* on a losing team, than *sit on the bench* for a winner. To enhance the team's chances for success, the coach should spend quality practice time working with all the players to improve their play. That should be a coach's primary, but indirect, commitment to winning.

HOW OLD IS OLD ENOUGH?

Pop Warner football, one of the oldest youth football organizations in existence today, requires that a child be 7 years old before the first of August in order to play. From my experience, seven can be a little too early for some children. Many of the 7-year-olds I've had on my teams are overwhelmed by most of things they face on the football field. The concentration span of a 7-year-old is often quite limited, and he or she can have difficulty understanding and remembering assignments. A team with many 7-year-olds will require several coaches with enormous patience and great imagination to keep the young players' attention. Many times even *that* is not enough. The danger, if the youngster is not physically or mentally ready, is that he or she will not enjoy the experience and will drop out before the season is over or will not play again the following year.

On the other hand, if a 7-year-old is confident and talented, that first year of experience will be a big advantage the following season when the child is eight. Given the choice, my recommendation would be to hold off one year unless the youngster is a very athletic and mature 7-year-old.

A TRAVELING TEAM OR AN INTRAMURAL TEAM?

In considering a program for your young football player, you may have a choice of either an intramural team or a traveling team. There a several important differences between the two.

Intramural teams play other teams within the local organization, and traveling teams play teams outside of the local organization, usually from neighboring communities.

Besides the travel involved, the biggest differences between the two situations are the level and intensity of competition on the field and in the stands. Traveling teams often attract better or more competitive players, more intense coaches and parents, and more overzealous fans. Winning could be the top priority for the opposition even if it is not for your team. The important thing to remember is that you may come up against some teams that do not share your local organization's philosophy about kids' sports.

A local intramural football program, on the other hand, typically has a philosophy that is shared by all its teams, coaches and parents. Fun is usually the priority. These programs usually have fewer players on a team, which means more playing time for each player, and also may have special playing rules to accommodate the broad spectrum of player skills and unusual player sizes.

An alignment of four or more teams in a particular age/weight division, with 15 players per team, playing each other three times a season is close to

ideal for an intramural program. The small size of
the squads guarantees extensive playing time.

Unfortunately, this configuration takes a fairly
large group of players with similar ages and weights,
a situation that many small organizations do not
have. Instead, they are forced to field a single traveling team with possibly 35 players. Playing time for
each player is quite limited, especially for the less
skilled player. This team has little control over the
behavior of the opposition's players, coaches or fans.
Nor does it have anything to say about the player's
age or weight grouping or about the rules under
which all the teams compete.

I have coached in both traveling and intramural
situations, and my own children played in both with
very positive football experiences in each. The intramural program, however, is my choice for most
younger kids, if it is available.

A number of years ago while living on Long
Island, I had an opportunity to create a different type
of intramural football program. Our organization at
that time had two strong intramural divisions, an
"over 90 pound" group and an "under 90 pound"
group with four teams in each division. In addition,
there were about 26 boys, age seven or eight, who
wanted to play but were very small and didn't really
fit well even in the "under 90 pound" division. To
accommodate these 26 players, a "Little Guys" program was formed. Each of the 26 players was issued
a red jersey and a blue jersey in addition to their
standard equipment. All these players would practice together as a group, twice a week. At practice,

the coaches would divide the players into two teams.
The kids would learn a few basic plays and some
basic defensive schemes and, on Saturday morning,
two teams, one wearing red jerseys, and one wearing
blue jerseys, would play each other.

The following week we would mix the kids up
and arrange two different teams from the group of
26. The kids played a different position each week.
Come Saturday these two different teams would play
each other. Some weeks a boy would play on the red
team, some weeks on the blue. All the kids played
both ways, on offense and on defense, and they all
played a lot because there were only 13 players on
each team. One of the coaches served as referee for
the game (very few penalties were called), and we
didn't keep score. The kids just played and had fun
with absolutely no pressure and little adult interfer-
ence. It was a very successful program, and the kids
and the parents both loved it.

While the right mix of players, in size and age,
is needed to implement such a program, it permits
a small or limited number of children to play in a
controlled situation within the local organization.
In our case it was much better than having these 26
youngsters play on a highly structured and more
competitive traveling team.

THE ORGANIZATION

Parents should consider, quite carefully, the priorities of the youth organization sponsoring their children's sports. I recently learned of an organization that has developed national guidelines for youth sports called the **National Alliance for Youth Sports (NAYS)**. Their philosophy is in complete alignment with my own. In 1987, the alliance created a uniform philosophy that youth sports programs should be based on the needs of the children, not the adults. The group identified a set of guiding principles or standards for the development and administration of children's sports programs. These eleven standards are reprinted as an appendix by permission of the NAYS and should be the foundation for all youth sports organizations.

In addition to endorsing principles such as those developed by the NAYS, the organization must be guided by a strong board of experienced directors who are dedicated to these principles and to the three important priorities of safety, fun and learning. The board should keep a watchful eye over each of the sports it provides to make certain that priorities do not change as good and experienced coaches or sport commissioners move out of the organization and new volunteers come in.

The organization should also, if possible, avoid a complete turnover of its board members in its periodic election process to ensure that the organization's philosophies are preserved. Many organizations keep a high-ranking officer on the board for one year following completion of his or her term of office. It is also helpful to have at least one board member who no longer has children active in the program. This individual will be familiar with the philosophies and goals of the organization and can be helpful in reconciling conflicts that may arise between parents of active players.

Good guidelines for children's sports programs can be quite fragile and must be protected and preserved by concerned parents and caring coaches.

"THE SAINT AND THE SINNER"

THE COACH

In looking for coaches, many youth organizations, even those with the best intentions, are often enamored with the win-loss record of coaching candidates or with the highest level at which the candidate played or coached. Organization officials should be more concerned about the new coach's philosophy regarding developing young players rather than how often his teams have won. Prior positive experience coaching kids is more important than where or at what level a candidate coached previously. The coaching challenge in little kids' football today is not in understanding and manipulating the Xs and Os. The challenge is to find coaches who believe the kids' enjoyment and development should take precedence over winning games and championships.

The ideal coach would have the patience of a saint, the wisdom of Solomon, the compassion of Christ, the commitment of a monk, the intuition of Dr. Benjamin Spock, the versatility of an actor, the skills of a teacher, the creativity of Walt Disney and the ego of a sleeping baby. The coach should also have a passion for little kids and for football.

Finding all these qualities in a single human being is understandably difficult. Still there are many wonderful coaches, men as well as women, serving youth programs throughout the country, doing an incredible job without all of the above attributes. What they do have is a passion for the game and for the kids. It's tough to go wrong as a coach if that's your starting point.

"ARE WE HAVING FUN YET?"

Studies have shown that as many as 70 percent of the children that participate in youth sports programs drop out before age 13. According to a recent survey, the main reasons kids drop out of sports are:
- players do not get a chance to play
- the coaches are abusive
- winning is overemphasized
- there is excessive repetition that leads to boredom
- players fear failure
- players face physical mismatches

Five of these drop-out factors are under the absolute and total control of the coach. So if the role of the youth football program is to provide its players a safe, enjoyable learning experience, then the individual coach's performance should be measured against each of these factors—not against a win-loss record. If the coach cannot measure up, he or she should not be coaching children, especially not the youngest age groups.

Now I know there are coaches who might argue their program is preparing its players for high school or college and that players who drop out for the above reasons should be weeded out anyway. That coach may add, "This is the real football world, and if your child is in it for fun, he or she is in the wrong program." At least the coach would be right on that score—it is the wrong program for most kids.

Some warning signs that should put you on guard when considering or observing youth football coaches include the following:
- The coach says, "My record in four years of coaching is 25 wins and 3 losses. I went to the playoffs every year."

- "I have a winning record wherever I've coached."
- The coach spends most of his time working with the best players and ignores the others.
- The coach curses, manhandles or harshly criticizes and demeans players for mistakes.
- The coach often argues with and berates game officials.
- The coach makes a special point of his technical expertise or his accomplishments as a former player.
- The coach talks more about the outcome of the game than the improvement of his players.
- More players are running laps or doing pushups for punishment than are participating in drills at the team's practice.
- Calisthenics and conditioning exercises are excessive, punishing and devoid of any element of fun, usually patterned after professional training camps.

Don't let my warnings about over-enthusiastic coaches put you off. There are many wonderful coaches working with young kids these days, and good programs are not hard to find. Take some time to talk to officials in the youth organization in your area. Meet the coaches, and find out their philosophy concerning little kids' sports. Try to observe the coach in action on the practice field or playing field. Better still, volunteer to be a coach. You'll have the time of your life and you will be able to affect team atmosphere.

THE COACH'S CODE OF CONDUCT

Nothing takes the fun out of a little kids' football game faster than an ugly sideline skirmish between two coaches or between a coach and an official. In no time at all, what starts as a disagreement between two adults escalates into a near riot among coaches, parents, officials and even players.

There is no excuse for this type of behavior at any time, in any sporting event. When it happens during a kids' game, it is more than irresponsible; it is deplorable, and what is worse, it is avoidable.

Sideline violence is much like a house fire. It starts with a small spark that slowly smolders, then increases quickly in intensity until it erupts, out of control, in full flame. Without the spark, there would be no fire. Coaches must realize they can be the catalyst to most sideline fires. Their behavior can ignite and incite others. It can also have the opposite effect. The coach's conduct can suffocate sparks in the process of developing.

A fundamental responsibility of any youth coach is to instill and encourage good sportsmanship in all members of the team. The coach must never lose sight of this goal. Players should be taught to play according to the rules and to respect the absolute authority of game officials. The coach who questions or argues a referee's call during a game, in full view of the players, is undermining this authority. Kids learn very quickly to follow the lead of their coach.

Penalties are a part of football, called by appointed officials to ensure that the game is played according to the rules. Most penalties are decisions of judgment

"WHADA YA MEAN HE WAS OFFSIDES???"

by the officials and are not eligible for dispute. For too many coaches, though, the yellow penalty flag is like the red cape of the matador to the bull—they see it and react. The best approach the coach can take regarding penalties is to simply ignore and accept them without discussion, and certainly without dispute or demonstration.

Often coaches will not only dispute or criticize a penalty called against their team, they demand to know which player committed the infraction so that the youngster can be promptly and publicly chastised. It is true that in the NFL, the referee identifies the guilty player, announcing his name, his number and the infraction over the public address system and on national television, but such action has no place in little kids' football. Players that incur penalties should not be singled out by the referee or the coach. They should remain anonymous. A sensitive and concerned coach will use this occasion to explain to the entire team the impact of the penalty and how to prevent it in the future. It is likely that most of the team needs and will benefit from such a reminder. In this way, all players can learn from the mistakes of their teammates.

If the coach is aware of which player committed the foul, he should follow up with that individual separately to make sure the youthful offender understands the penalty and how to avoid it in the future. Few kids can withstand, without emotional distress, the verbal and often personal abuse that is heaped upon them by an irate or insensitive coach.

The attitude of the coach toward game officials directly and dramatically affects the attitudes and conduct of the assistant coaches, the players and the fans. The coach who does not get excited or upset by penalties sends a positive message to everyone and minimizes inappropriate behavior on the field, on the sidelines and in the stands. By doing otherwise, the coach is behaving irresponsibly and is risking trouble.

The coach must also act as facilitator to prevent problems from starting. If there are potentially unruly or overbearing assistant coaches or parents on the sidelines, the wise coach will tactfully remind them that the players are little kids trying to have fun.

A Coach's Code of Conduct
- Always be a positive influence for players, other coaches and parents
- Always take control of your sidelines and your fans
- Always praise both teams for their effort
- Always balance criticism with praise
- Always give each player a fair and full measure of play
- Always provide each player with the best possible instruction
- Never let your desire to win interfere with any of the three priorities (safety, fun, learning)
- Never dispute or criticize a penalty or an official's decision
- Never ridicule a player or an official
- Never use profanity, alcohol or tobacco on the athletic field

The National Youth Sports Coaches Association, a division of the National Alliance for Youth Sports, discussed earlier, also has its own Coaches' Code of Conduct similar to this. It is included below because it provides even further guidance and greater depth into a youth coach's responsibilities. I endorse it most enthusiastically.

National Youth Sport Coaches Association Coaches' Code of Conduct

I will place the emotional and physical well-being of my players ahead of a personal desire to win. Expected Behavior:

1. Using appropriate language in appropriate tones when interacting with players, league officials, game officials, parents and spectators.

2. Including all players in team activities without regard to race, religion, color, sex, sexual orientation, body type, national origin, ancestry, disability, ability, or any other legally protected classification.

3. Treating all players, league officials, game officials, parents and spectators with dignity and respect.

4. Playing all players according to the equal participation rules established by the league and the spirit if those rules.

5. Encouraging youth to participate in other sports and activities to promote all aspects of their development.

6. Allowing reaasonable absences from practice.

I will treat each player as an individual, remembering the large range of emotional and physical development for the same age group.
Expected Behavior:

1. Recognizing the differences of each child and treating each player as an individual while demonstrating concern for each individual's needs and well-being.

2. Encouraging all players, regardless of skill level, to be included as members of the team and to remain involved in sports.

3. Recognizing that some physical tasks, drills and demands are not appropriate for all youth.

4. Recognizing that youth may vary greatly in physical, social and emotional maturation and considering these factors when setting up competitions and when interacting with youth.

I will do my best to provide a safe playing situation for my players.
Expected Behavior:

1. Maintaining a high level of awareness of potentially unsafe conditions.

2. Protecting players from sexual molestation, assault, physical or emotional abuse.

3. Correcting or avoiding unsafe practice or playing conditions.

4. Using appropriate safety equipment necessary to protect players.

5. Seeing that all players are provided with adequate adult supervision while under the coach's care.

I will promise to review and practice the basic first aid principles needed to treat injuries of my players.

Expected Behavior:

1. Keeping basic first aid supplies available in all practice and game situations.

2. Recognizing and administering proper first aid to an injured player.

3. Demonstrating concern for an injured player, notifying parents and cooperating with medical authorities.

4. Protecting the players' well-being by removing them from activity when injured and not returning them to activity if they are compromised by injury.

I will do my best to organize practices that are fun and challenging for all my players.

Expected Behavior:

1. Establishing practice plans that are interesting, varied, productive and aimed at improving all players' skills and individual abilities.

2. Devoting appropriate time to the individual improvement of each player.

3. Conducting practices of reasonable length and intensity appropriate for the age and conditioning of the players.

I will lead by example in demonstrating fair play and sportsmanship to all my players.

Expected Behavior:

1. Adopting the position, teaching and demonstrating that it is our basic moral code to treat others as we would like to be treated.

2. Abiding by and supporting the rules of the game as well as the spirit of the rules.

3. Providing an environment conducive to fair and equitable competition.

4. Using the influential position of youth coach as an opportunity to promote, teach and expect sportsmanship and fair play.

I will provide a sports environment for my team that is free of drugs, tobacco and alcohol, and I will refrain from their use at all youth sports events.
Expected Behavior:

1. Being alcohol and drug free at all team activities or in the presence of players.

2. Refraining from the use of any type of tobacco products at all team activities or in the presence of players.

3. Encouraging parents to refrain from the public use of tobacco products or alcohol at team activities.

I will be knowledgeable in the rules of each sport that I coach, and I will teach these rule to my players.
Expected Behavior:

1. Becoming knowledgeable, understanding and supportive of all applicable game rules, league rules, regulations and policies.

2. Teaching and requiring compliance of these rules among players.

I will use those coaching techniques appropriate for each of the skills that I teach.
Expected Behavior:

1. Teaching techniques that reduce the risk of injury to both the coach's own players and their opponents.

2. Discouraging illegal contact or intentional dangerous play and administering swift and equitable discipline to players involved in such activity.

I will remember that I am a youth sports coach, and that the game is for children and not adults.
Expected Behavior:

1. Maintaining a positive, helpful and supportive attitude.

2. Exercising your authority/influence to control the behavior of the fans and spectators.

3. Exhibiting gracious acceptance of defeat or victory.

4. Accepting and adhering to all league rules and policies related to the participation of adults and youth.

5. Fulfilling the expected role of a youth coach to adopt a "children first" philosophy.

6. Allowing and encouraging the players to listen, learn and play hard within the rules.

7. Placing the emphasis on fun and participation.

If all youth coaches faithfully followed these Codes of Conduct, youth sports would be fun, players would enjoy playing and sideline violence at children's sporting events would not occur. It is up to the coaches and parents to make it happen.

"I'VE SEEN SHORTER LINES
AT DISNEY WORLD"

WINNING VS. SUCCESS

The coach of a little kids' team needs to have a definition of success that is not predicated on a winning season. Players and coaches alike need to understand that participation, performance, effort and improvement count as much, if not more, than the final score of any kids' game. The old expression "It's not whether you win or lose but how you play the game" is much preferred over the more modern Vince Lombardi adage that "Winning isn't everything. It's the only thing." By the way, if Coach Lombardi were alive today, I believe he would certainly qualify his remark to exclude little kids' games.

Perhaps winning is the yardstick for success because it is so easy to measure. If your team scores more points than the other team, you win. If not, you lose. Still, coaches of children's sports should avoid making a big deal out of winning or losing and focus instead on how well the players performed or how much they have improved since the last game. Very often in competitive sports, winning or losing results from situations beyond the players' control. An official's judgment, timing, good or bad breaks or funny bounces of the ball may determine who wins. In professional sports, the bottom line is winning. As they say, "A win is a win, no matter how ugly." Not so in kids' games. Participation and performance should be the bottom line.

In kids' games, playing and competing are the important measures. A losing effort by a kids' team that plays well may still be a great success, although the success is more difficult to quantify. A game is a

"THE WALL"

success if the players all had fun and all felt they contributed to making the game exciting. A coach, in turn, is successful if all his players have fun and improve throughout the season, two very subjective assessments. In order for a coach to be successful, all his players must experience a full and fair measure of play, not just some minimum required number of plays at a position that hides the player from significant competition. Of course, not all players can participate on every play of every game, but they should play enough to feel they have contributed and they should be allowed to play some plays at a position they enjoy. In short, then, success in kids' sports is measured by the players' enjoyment, their improvement and their contribution. Even though success may be difficult to quantify, the players will understand when they experience it. Kids know fun when they have it!

Practice time is an important part of the full measure of play idea. All players should be involved through out practice. Players should not stand around waiting extended periods for their turns at a drill or in a scrimmage. Keep drill groups small, and rotate players into scrimmage every two or three plays.

The coach can have a real influence on the way players feel about their assigned position. The coach does it through trial, recognition, praise and instruction and by letting the player practice at several positions. Usually if a player performs well at a position, he or she likes it. If a player doesn't perform well at one, he or she dislikes it. Or conversely, if a player doesn't like a position, he or she probably won't perform well there. Through this try-and-succeed

"THE MOLE"

"THE WAFFLE"

process, along with the coach's guidance and positive feedback, players "find" positions where they are comfortable and happy.

Creative nicknames can also be used to make players feel good about their positions and about themselves. Nicknames add an element of fun to the game and give players an identity. Nicknames make kids feel extra-special. Football fans everywhere know the Pittsburgh Steelers' powerful running back is called "The Bus" even if they may not know his real name is Jerome Bettis. Kids love to be given nicknames. When a small defensive lineman learns to stay low and successfully burrow under larger offensive blockers into the backfield, the player might earn the nickname "The Mole." The name itself is not especially complimentary, but as recognition of an accomplishment it is distinctive and considered an honor. Our kicker is called "The Big Toe," or "Big Foot," the fast little runner might be "The Wiz" or "The Jet," and the heavy and slow defensive tackle "The Wall."

Kids enjoy creative characterization of their accomplishments, too. When an offensive blocker puts his opponent "flat on his back" on the ground, we say the blocker got a pancake. If the blocker not only flattens, but runs over his opponent and gets a second block, that's called a waffle, so named because of the imaginary cleat marks or holes the blocker leaves in the pancaked player's stomach during the run-over. Kody, our offensive tackle, couldn't wait to get back to the huddle during a scrimmage so he could tell me, "Coach, I got two pancakes and a waffle already! Did you see them?"

"FUN/NO FUN"

These things all contribute to making football a fun and exciting experience for young players. How can you tell if the team is having fun? Some direct and indirect measures include the following:

- If the kids don't want practice to end or are disappointed when it does, you can be sure they are having fun.
- If kids are missing practice regularly, there is a good chance they are not enjoying it. The coach should find out why.
- If the kids remain upbeat after losing a game or talk about the positive things they did, they probably had fun.
- If some kids come to practice but complain often that they want to sit out because don't feel good, they're probably are not having fun.
- If kids are enthusiastic about a particular drill or practice routine, they enjoy it. If they gripe or moan about a drill, or don't make much of an effort in doing it, it's probably no fun, and the coach should try to spice it up or eliminate it.
- Kids who are laughing and smiling are having fun.
- If more than several kids quit the team, you can be sure it is not a fun time. Find out why fast.

"ONE OF LIFE'S
EMBARRASSING MOMENTS"

INSTANT REPLAY

THE LAUGHS AND THE LESSONS

This section, as its title suggests, is a look back at seasons past. It's a glimpse at some of the funny and unbelievable things kids do and say. These experiences recap many of the things I've learned through the years, mostly from the kids, on how to coach them and what to expect and not expect from them. It is the essence of this book.

Some of the funny situations described may be difficult to believe but they all really happened as reported. The stories and the kids are real. That these events actually occurred is what makes them so profound and so memorable. I am grateful I was there and within earshot. I regret that I don't have a video recording to replay.

My absolute favorite story about little kids playing football is about an 8-year-old boy named Adam who played in our youngest intramural football program 20 or so years ago. Adam was an enthusiastic youngster who enjoyed sports in general and football in particular. He was a bright, scholarly type, extremely articulate, with thick horned-rimmed glasses. He reminds me a lot of Ogilvy in *The Bad News Bears*, except Adam may have been slightly more athletic.

Adam, who had never played running back

before, couldn't wait for a chance as quarterback; an opportunity, as his coach, I had promised him as soon as he could run at least three plays.

That day finally came, and Adam started the game at quarterback for the Blue team. For most of the first half, he struggled with the center snap and with handoffs and did little worth reporting. To make things easier for him, and to avoid a fumble (the ball was on our own 10-yard line), I advised a quarterback sneak for his next play.

Much to my surprise and even more to Adam's, he broke away from the line of scrimmage and into the secondary. Adam was taller than most of the players, could run pretty well and appeared headed for a long gain at least. When he crossed our 20-yard line, he had built up a good head of steam . . . I couldn't believe it, but Adam was on his way to a 90-yard touchdown. The defense was in hot pursuit but falling behind fast.

Disaster struck, however, as he crossed midfield. Adam's pants started to slip down. He struggled to hitch them back up without losing control of the ball and continued toward the end zone as fast as he could run under the circumstances. By the time he reached the other team's 30-yard line, the pants had dropped below his knees and his speed had dropped seriously, too. What was even worse, the defenders were closing the gap.

At the 10, with his pants at his ankles, dignity prevailed. Adam stopped, put the ball down and tried to pull up the problem pants using both hands. Before he could regain control of the ball and his pants, he was smothered by a horde of defenders.

When the pile was sorted out, Adam was ruled down 8 yards short of a touchdown. I didn't know whether to laugh or cry. I think I did both. I'll never forget it, and I'm sure Adam and his parents never will either.

Obviously, all kids are not created equal. As a coach you can expect your team will have a wide range of talent, and most of your players will not be superstars. Part of the fun and reward for the coach is seeing "ordinary" first-year players improve and develop into good runners, blockers or tacklers as the season progresses. Remember the words of that wise coach, "Everyone can't do everything, but everyone can do something." It's the coach's job to work with all players, putting them in positions that match their abilities and conducting drills that help them improve. The more they improve, the better they feel about themselves, and the more fun they will have.

Perhaps the only other safe thing to say about expectations is for a coach not to have any. Just take things as they come. For example, don't expect your players to know very much about the game they will be playing. You'll probably be disappointed if you do.

An alternative suggestion might be to expect almost anything because anything is likely to happen. Since I've coached little kids' football teams for more than 30 years, I thought I'd seen just about everything. But I was taken completely by surprise at the start of a Pop Warner Mighty Mite practice this past year. Devin, a really quick running back came

"A COACH SHOULD BE PREPARED
TO DEAL WITH ANYTHING!"

up to me with his helmet in his hand. He obviously had some kind of problem. "Would you please help me coach?" he asked. I said, "Sure, Devin, what's the trouble?" He said, "Would you please take my earring out for me?" Now I'm not sure when or how it came about that little boys started wearing earrings. All I know is that most youth leagues do not allow players to wear jewelry in games . . . thank goodness.

Coaches should prepare for practice ahead of time. They should have a detailed plan for things they want to accomplish. They should expect their players to come to practice on time and properly equipped. But getting kids to show up for practice on time can be a continuing problem for a coach. It is practically impossible, short of dire threats, to have an entire team on hand when practice is scheduled to start. *That you can expect.*

You might not think that players' having the proper equipment would be a problem especially if the league issues equipment. But it is, and all too often. A few years ago, Bobby came to practice fully prepared to play with his shoulder pads, arm pads, hand pads, pants, neck roll, the whole nine yards . . . everything but his helmet, which he had left in the car. A week or so later, Joe came to practice missing his pants. I was a little surprised, but our center, Jake, thought it was hilarious and carried on about it for nearly five minutes. The next practice Bobby managed to remember his helmet and Joe had his pants, but Jake showed up without his shoes! Not the wrong shoes . . . no shoes, just socks. I don't know how that happens. Don't most

"WE'RE READY TO PLAY, COACH"

people wear shoes when they go outside some place? Maybe it only happens in Florida. It never happened on Long Island.

Quite often, kids come to practice without their pants. I don't mean no pants at all. I mean their football pants. They have a pair of shorts or regular pants on instead and usually offer the excuse that "My Mom washed 'em, and they're not dry yet."

Poor Mom. She always seems to be the scapegoat, if you believe the kids. When kids are late for practice, it is always Mom's fault. When they come without some important piece of equipment, Mom has it in her car or put it somewhere. One of the best Mom excuses I've ever heard came from a player that missed a scrimmage game. "I couldn't come to the game Saturday; I had to go to Disney World," Dylan said. When I looked at him with a fishy eye, he added, "Honest, coach, my Mom made me go."

Whatever the situation, kids always have interesting excuses. Joey missed practice one Tuesday. When I saw him Thursday at the next practice, I asked him where he'd been. "I couldn't come," he said. "I had to get a hair cut." I guess my earlier comments on commitment and priorities to Joey and the team had missed the mark.

At practice one night Nick was having trouble running plays through the correct hole. I suspected that he hadn't read the playbook I'd given him, so I asked him if he had. "I was going to, coach, but the baby ate it." I think I used that excuse when I was a kid except, as I recall, it was the dog that ate my homework.

As far as expectations are concerned, the Boy Scouts

"HONEST, COACH. MY MOM MADE ME GO!"

have the right idea. "Be Prepared" . . . for anything!

A coach should not be surprised by anything he sees on the playing field when kids are involved nor should he assume anything. I learned this lesson my very first year coaching little kids. It was the spring of 1966 at one of my first baseball practices as coach of the Dinosaurs. The players were 8 years old and in their first year of baseball. We had a broad range of talent on the Dino's but it was easy to see that Mike was our best player. Mike could hit, catch, field and throw and knew all the rules of the game. Most of the other players were a step or two below Mike. It was also easy to see that, at the opposite end of the spectrum, was a little boy named Hunter.

Hunter apparently had managed to avoid any exposure whatsoever to baseball in his first 8 years on earth. He knew nothing about the game and had never even picked up a bat before. Of course, I didn't know that at the time.

This day, I was pitching batting practice, and the boys who weren't hitting or on deck were in the field. It was Hunter's turn at bat, and after about a dozen or more pitches, he was told to run out the next ball he hit.

A few pitches later he actually made contact and rolled the ball out in front of the plate. It took some encouragement, but he finally ran to first. I told him to stay at first as a base runner. Mike was the next batter, and he hit every ball pitched, strike or not. After six or seven hard-hit balls, Mike got his chance to run one out.

He hit the next pitch like a shot right at the shortstop, Johnny, who was making roads in the

"IT'S VERY DRY WITHOUT MILK ON THE SIDE."

"AN AIRTIGHT INFIELD"

dirt for his imaginary cars. The ball whizzed past Johnny unnoticed and rolled all the way to the school parking lot.

Hunter stood dutifully on first as originally instructed. Mike was thinking "home run" but knew he couldn't pass Hunter, so he screamed for him to run. I joined in yelling at Hunter to run to second. He did, and Mike followed closely behind, careful not to pass him. When Hunter stopped at second, we all yelled for him to go to third. He did as directed and once again stopped on the bag. When I yelled, "Go home, Hunter! Go home!" he left the base and headed toward the plate but veered off at the last second and got on his bike. Dumbfounded, I asked, "Where are you going, Hunter?" "Home," he said, without hesitation. I still have a hard time believing this event actually happened, but I saw it with my own eyes. Six years later, a fictional character named Amelia Bedelia re-enacted Hunter's faux pas on the pages of Peggy Parish's entertaining children's book, *Play Ball, Amelia Bedelia*, thus supporting the theory that "art imitates life."

This drove home two important lessons for me. First, don't ever assume your kids know anything about the game you are coaching. Some may; others may not. Things you take for granted, kids may not understand.

The other lesson is most important to remember when working with kids. Words can be a source of great confusion. They may mean one thing to you and nothing or something completely different to a kid, as they did with Hunter. You may have heard about the little boy who asked his first baseball coach

"GO HOME, HUNTER"

what to do after he hit the ball. Without thinking, the coach responded, "You just hit the ball and run to me." Sure enough, the boy hit the ball and followed his coach's directions explicitly. He ran to the coach who was coaching at third base. It's an amusing story, but the humor ceased when the coach chastised the child for doing such a dumb thing.

We need to remember that little kids are just that—little kids. They are not small or undersized adults. They can be easily confused by directions that are not clear or concise. That rule is probably true for most adults, too, but with kids, it is especially so. Most kids have a limited vocabulary and usually don't understand clichés or technical sports jargon. Many of the things that coaches say fall in the category of jargon or "jock speak" and often don't make any sense at all. Do little kids really understand "bear down," "suck it up" or "bow your neck"?

Also, kids may have limited physical capabilities or coordination. Many have yet to learn to do things adults do without thinking. Kids' practices are often new, strange and sometimes threatening or frightening situations for some youngsters. For children struggling to master new skills while trying to understand confusing directions, practice can be overwhelming. The mantra "Keep It Simple" is key to any successful learning experience . . . for a kids' coach, it is an absolute must.

All too often, coaches treat their players like they were adults, either by the way they talk to the kids or by what they expect from them. I've been guilty of this more than once myself.

I was reminded of this very recently while show-

"WHICH WAY IS UP?"

ing my 8-year-old Pop Warner team how the offensive blockers should line up at the line of scrimmage. It's a two-dimensional problem for them. They must line up on the ball without being offsides, and they need to take the proper splits or spaces between blockers. Kids typically have trouble positioning themselves correctly. If a player is not in the right spot, the coaches usually tell him or her to move in or out, up or back, as necessary.

This wouldn't be a problem for an adult but I've seen kids get confused by directions of this sort before. So to make sure the players understood what we meant when we said "move in," "move out," "move up" or "move back," I asked Ryan, our left end, to point in the direction he would move if we told him to "move in" (towards the ball). He thought a bit, then correctly pointed to his right. He again correctly pointed to the left for "move out" and to the rear for "move back." But he thought for quite a while about "move up" so I asked him, "Ryan, which way is up?" With a puzzled expression, he finally pointed to the sky. We all laughed, but the message was clear. It was a poor choice of words, a confusing question for an 8-year-old. Everyone knows which way up is!

Words got in the way on another occasion recently. I shouldn't have been surprised when Logan, our 8-year-old quarterback rolled out around right end for a long gain at practice one night. After all, Logan is a very talented little football player. What puzzled me was that Logan was told to run a quarterback sneak, not a rollout. Asked about the mix-up when he returned to the huddle, Logan

"HIT 'EM HARD, MIKEY!"

admitted that, indeed, the play I called was a sneak, but he explained that I also told him to "go to the right side of the center." He interpreted that to mean sweep right. So you see, even the best players can be confused by what are meant to be helpful directions from the coach.

No matter how hard coaches try to keep things simple, confusion can creep in. Once when we were practicing a blocking drill, Mikey, our smallest and probably least aggressive player, was matched up against Jack, who was not only a little bigger but considerably more aggressive. Mikey was having difficulty moving Jack and wasn't putting much pop into his block. Our coach took Mikey aside and showed him again how to fire out from his three-point stance and how to bring his hands up to push against Jack. After a few more blocks that were a little more forceful but still too soft, the coach pleaded, "That's better, Mikey, but this time I want you to hit him hard! . . . I mean really hit him hard!" Mikey followed these directions to the letter. He fired out of his three-point stance and delivered a solid right cross to Jack's shoulder pads that Evandor Holyfield would have admired. So much for "hit 'em hard!"

Football players have much to learn before they can play a game. The players must master special skills like blocking and tackling. In addition, they must also learn the responsibilities of their positions and what to do on specific plays. Here again the simple approach is the best. Offensive plays are typically characterized by a set of two numbers. The numbers represent locations or holes in the offensive

"DID HE SAY POWER SLANT 32-DOUBLE
ZIG ZAG RIGHT ON 2 OR ON 3?"

line and are also used to identify the ball carrier.
Holes on the right side of the offensive center are
numbered 2, 4, 6 and 8; on the left side of the center,
they are 1, 3, 5 and 7 as shown. The quarterback is
given the number 1, the left halfback the number 2,
the fullback the number 3 and the right halfback the
number 4 (assuming a straight T-formation). A play
is identified by combining the number of the back
who is to carry the ball with the number of the hole
through which he is to run. If the fullback, #3, is to
run the ball through the #2 hole, the play is called 32.
It sounds a little confusing, but most of the kids pick
it up pretty fast. Sometimes I augment the play
number with a name like "blast," "dive" or "sweep"
or even add the ball carrier's name to the play, as in
"Mike's Dive Right 32" as a reminder. The simpler,
the better.

7 E 5 T 3 G 1 C 2 G 4 T 6 E 8

1

2   4

3

The numbers diagram

- numbered holes

This numbering system is fairly common in midget football and is also used at higher levels of play. As I said, most 8-, 9- or 10-year-old kids are able to deal with it. It may take some time, but they can usually learn their plays. 7-year-olds, on the other hand, often have difficulty with this concept. These players may need very simple directions like "you get the ball and run between Joey and Bobby." Better still, try to use these kids on defense where things are not as complicated. Next year they may be more ready for the complexities of offense.

THE THREE DS OF COACHING LITTLE KIDS

As in teaching most things, the three Ds are a good method for the coach to follow. They are:
- Describe
- Demonstrate
- Drill

The description should be limited to a short and simple explanation of the task to be learned. Don't overdo the talking part or the kids will get bored or lost in the words.

Demonstrate the technique in the simplest way. Don't clutter up the demonstration with anything extra. Try to avoid unnatural movements. Avoid demonstrating the incorrect way of doing something, if possible. Kids often lose the "don't" part of "don't do it this way" and think you are showing them the right way to do something.

Sometimes it is necessary to physically assist the player with the technique. For example, most kids initially have some difficulty getting into a good three-point stance, even after you've told them what to do and showed them the proper stance. It may be necessary for the coach to help them position their feet correctly or move their hands to the right spot. Be careful, though, not to manhandle the players. Adults can be awfully intimidating to youngsters. Also avoid leading a player around by the face mask, even if it *is* a convenient handle. Kids really don't like it, and neither do their parents.

On this subject of intimidation, let me make a rec-ommendation that helps coaches communicate more

"GETTING DOWN TO THEIR LEVEL"

easily with little kids. Try to get down to their level whenever you have something important to say to them. Do it by getting down on one knee, a common football position. This way you bring the discussion down to their level, so to speak. The kids seem to pay attention better if you are eye-to-eye with them.

As a matter of necessity, most coaches spend a great deal of time correcting young players' mistakes. With kids, it is very important that the coach be especially careful with criticism. Try to remember to critique the player's behavior, the technique or the execution, not the player himself. If possible, try to put negative criticism in positive terms. For example, if a blocker didn't block his man very effectively you might say, "That was a pretty good block, Jeff. You had your hands in exactly the right position. Now try stepping out with your right foot first, instead of your left. You'll be in a better position to move him out of the hole." Negative criticism is best given in combination with praise. Think of it as recipe: "An ounce of criticism should be mixed with a pound or two of praise." In this way the player's self-image is not diminished.

Use humorous or visual descriptions to illustrate points whenever possible, but be careful not to ridicule anyone. Once we told our kids "We don't want any frogs around here. No Kermits, please. We are the Panthers!" to remind them to avoid the frog-like position they sometimes took instead of a good three-point stance. Fortunately, there weren't any boys named Kermit on our team, or it could have been embarrassing for the child and the coaches.

If there are girls on the team be careful to avoid

"NO FROGS, PLEASE"

using demeaning "girl" language such as referring to someone as a sissy or saying such things as "he throws just like a girl."

Reinforce the description and the demonstration with as many different types of drills as possible. Do these drills regularly at practice, but keep them fresh and varied to avoid boredom. Most young kids have short attention spans, and during extended periods of mental or physical inactivity their minds and bodies can wander in all sorts of directions. Some react by fooling around or chatting with a teammate; others just drift off to some imaginary place in space. There was a boy named Jimmy on my first baseball team who, when things got boring in the outfield, would take off his baseball hat, put it over his face and study the drifting cloud formations through the holes in his cap for an entire inning. Coaches need to keep kids busy and participating, or they may drift off like Jimmy.

Always start with the basics. Again, don't assume your players have any knowledge of what you are discussing. I always make a point of asking my team of first-year players at an early practice session, what the words "Offense" and "Defense" mean to them. I am no longer surprised that most kids don't know the difference between the two terms at the beginning of the season. This lack of knowledge, of course, is a real challenge because players have to tackle on defense and block on offense, two completely different tasks and concepts. They are often confused whether they are playing on offense or on defense and need to be reminded. It is not unusual to see two players, one on offense and the other on defense,

"WATCHING THE CLOUDS GO BY"

blocking each other. I have a vivid memory of our offensive guard, Dave, blocking his opposite number in a game many years ago. The play was over, and the two combatants continued to lean hard against each other although neither player was moving his feet. Even after the whistle had blown, the two continued to lean against each other. They looked like two mountain rams with their horns locked in combat.

Kids sometimes have trouble with terminology in sports. A 7-year-old youngster, playing in the first football game of his life, asked me early in the first half, how many more *innings* were left to play. Also, most first-year kids don't know the names of the different positions in football. Ask them, and you will hear things like the "way back," "the catcher" or "the hiker." True, they will learn positions quickly, but sometimes little Mike, your fullback, will forget which one the fullback is or where he should line up.

The coach should ask a lot of questions during drills and other instructive sessions to find out how much each player is actually understanding. If you get the 1,000-yard stare in response, start again.

Try to watch each player sometime during drills, scrimmages and game situations. Oftentimes the lesson of the drill doesn't carry over to the game situation. I remember the first time I watched little Josh, one of our 7-year-old defensive backs, in a scrimmage. Before the play started, he took up his position properly, about 6 yards from the line of scrimmage. But when the quarterback called "Ready-Set," Josh got into a three-point stance.

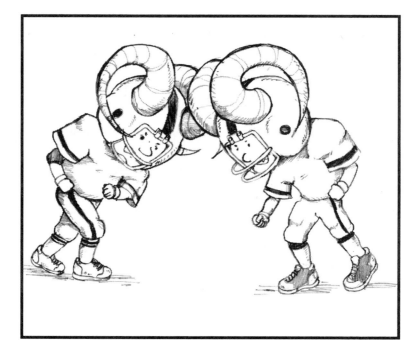

"IS IT TIME TO GO BACK
TO THE HUDDLE YET?"

When the quarterback said "Hut 1," Josh stood straight up, turned around and ran straight back into his own end zone as fast as he could. I didn't know whether he was trying to get as far away from the play as possible or whether he was running for a touchdown but forgot to get the ball. It took Josh a long time to understand that the defensive back should come up and make the tackle.

TEAM BUILDING:
MATCHING PLAYERS AND POSITIONS

Football is, in my mind, the ultimate team game, and building players into a team is one of the coach's most important and rewarding tasks. The coach must put players into positions they are capable of playing and then must teach them how to play those positions.

The aggressive kids may try to play two or three positions all at the same time. The ones who are less aggressive may shy away from even their own area of responsibility. For the team to be successful, each player must do his or her job on every play or at least on most plays. Aggressive players must learn to "stay home" in their assigned positions. The less-than-aggressive ones need to be encouraged to play harder in their spaces. Once the players understand their roles, teamwork starts to develop. The runners learn that offensive linemen help them run by opening holes. Linebackers learn that defensive linemen can shield them from blockers. Defensive ends learn to turn sweeps inside so that linebackers or defensive backs can make tackles. When these things happen on a regular basis, you have built a team.

Position Station Drills are helpful in matching a player to a position. The coach should also try to consider the player's preference, if it isn't an obvious mismatch with the player's skills. But that can be a problem because not many kids know, when they start out, what a right guard is, let alone want to be one.

Some kids are made to play on defense, and others are better suited to offense. For example, the younger or less mature players in a group may have difficulty understanding some of the concepts on offense such as snap count, play numbers, hole numbers and blocking assignments but may do well on the defensive line where the only thing they need to understand is: "Watch the ball, and when it moves, tackle the person who has it."

Whether they play on offense or defense, kids can get confused if they are moved around from position to position. Even a simple change, from right tackle to left tackle, for example, can be a challenge for a youngster because the hole numbers on the left side of the ball are different from the hole numbers on the right. Usually it is best to leave a player in an assigned position for several games. After all, it takes more than a few practices and some playing time in games to really learn what to do or how to react in different situations at a position.

As for playing both ways, first-time players can get confused over whether they should be blocking or tackling when moved back and forth from offense to defense. Some leagues may restrict two-way players. It may be more difficult for the players and the coaches, but I think kids like to have a chance to play both ways in the same game. For this reason, sometime toward the end of the season, we will switch offensive and defensive players around in practice and, if the kids show enthusiasm, even in a game.

The important thing to remember about players and positions is to try and put players in positions where they can do well. If a position is too difficult or requires different skills or abilities, players get frustrated and discouraged, and the fun will go out of football for them. Put them in positions they can handle, and they'll enjoy the game.

POSITION STATION DRILLS

Position Station Drills are very important for several reasons, especially in the younger playing levels where kids are playing football for the first time. Position Station Drills introduce players to each of the eight primary position categories, the names of the positions, the responsibilities of the positions and some of the fundamental techniques and movements involved with each. The eight basic positions are: center, offensive lineman, defensive lineman, quarterback, running back, receiver, linebacker and defensive back. Further breakdown of the basic positions such as fullback and defensive end are handled at specialty position stations at later practices.

Young kids and first-year players may be familiar with some of the higher profile positions from watching games on television but have little understanding of the skills necessary to play those positions or the responsibilities entailed. As explained earlier, most of the kids don't yet know the difference between offense and defense, let alone the names of the positions.

Exposing all players to each position station during the first several practices allows them all to actively experience some of the basic elements of every position and see firsthand what it takes to play there.

When coaches can observe players in every position and evaluate their potential at each spot, they are better able to find the right position for each player.

Position Station Drills are performed at the initial practice sessions early in the season and may be done first without equipment and then with equipment. The specific drills will vary as a result. The elements of each station are described below. Some coaches may prefer techniques other than the ones I've described. If they work, fine. These approaches have worked well for little kids in the past.

Quarterback Station
1. Starting position
   - head up
   - hands under center, top hand pushing against the center's bottom, lower hand forms a V with base of the palm touching the top hand
   - shoulders parallel with the line of scrimmage
   - knees flexed
   - feet pointing straight ahead
   - look to the left and the right to check linemen
2. Cadence or Snap Count
   - loud, deliberate and not hurried "Ready" (delay 2 seconds)
   "Set" (delay 2 seconds)
   "Hut 1" (short delay)
   "Hut 2" (short delay)
   "Hut 3"

The 2-second delay after "Ready" and "Set" is needed because kids in their haste often shout the "Ready, Set, Hut" too quickly, not giving their offensive linemen a chance to get set before the ball is snapped. The quarterback should say "Hut-1," "Hut-2," "Hut-3" not just "Hut"-"Hut"-"Hut" because kids may forget which "Hut" was which if the snap is on three.

3. Handoffs and Fakes
   - keep two hands on the ball
   - keep the ball close to the body except when

"THE QUARTERBACK"

making the handoff or fake
- on a handoff put the ball firmly into the runner's "pocket" (the open space between the player's arms) with both hands and feel it nestle against the runner's stomach as he or she closes down on the ball
- follow through as play requires
- on a fake or ride, keep two hands on the ball; one hand on the front of the ball and one hand on the back (not on the top and bottom) so that it won't be knocked out during the fake
- turn and step in the direction of the handoff or fake. Mastering the footwork is difficult for more than a few kids, especially when trying to coordinate the feet with the hands. It is best if the player can work his way through this naturally, without a lot of detailed instruction.

4. Perform Cadence, Handoff and Fake Drills

Running Back Station

1. Starting Position
   - 3-point stance, feet and eyes pointing straight ahead
   - approximately 4 yards from the line of scrimmage.
2. Taking the Handoff
   - make a pocket using both arms and stomach, and close down on the ball with both hands
   - don't try to take the ball in your hands
   - don't stop at the quarterback to take the ball; run through the handoff to the hole

"THE RUNNING BACK"

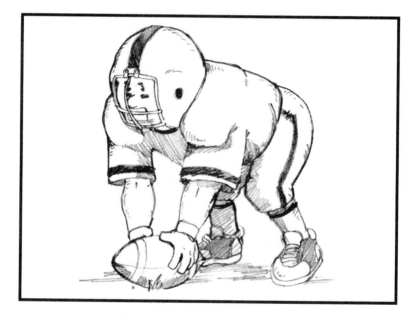

"THE CENTER"

3. Running with the Ball
   - run in a low position, not straight up
   - keep both hands on the ball until through the hole and into open field
   - keep one point of the ball cupped in your hand and the other point tucked into your armpit
   - in the open field, carry the ball in the arm farthest away from the pursuing tacklers
4. Receiving a Fake Handoff
   - run in a low position
   - do not close down on the ball when the quarterback puts it in your stomach
   - after the fake, stay low and run as hard as if you had the ball
5. Run Handoff and Fake Drills
6. Run the Staggered Cone Course

Offensive Center Station
(The center should be a taller player if possible. Very short players wind up too low to the ground, forcing the quarterback to bend over severely. This makes a good exchange difficult.)
1. Starting Position
   - both hands on the ball, head up, rear end up, knees slightly bent, back almost level, feel the quarterback's hands pushing against your bottom
2. On the Snap Count
   - move the ball up to the quarterback's hands very hard and fast, try to sting the quarterback's hands. During the snap, the ball should be turned 90 degrees so that the laces are

"THE OFFENSIVE LINEMAN"

parallel to the line of scrimmage when the ball reaches the quarterback's hands.
- start the ball back on the "HU" sound of "Hut," don't wait until the quarterback says the number
- hold the ball in that position until the quarterback takes it, don't throw it up

3. After the Snap
- when the quarterback has taken the ball, fire out on your block, but remember your first responsibility is to get the ball to the quarterback

Offensive Lineman Station

1. Starting Position
- 3-point stance, balanced position, feet as wide apart as the shoulders, head up, back nearly level, one hand on the ground forming a triangle with the feet

2. Fire Out on the Snap Count
- step first in the direction of the player to be blocked
- fire out low, rising up, do not stand up
- keep feet in a wide base, and use short choppy steps
- bring hands up under opponent's shoulder pads using an open palm and drive him out of the hole
- maintain block until the whistle blows

3. Learn the Blocking Priorities—GOL
- G=inside gap
- O=man over
- L=linebacker

4. Dummy Blocking Drill

"THE DEFENSIVE LINEMAN"

Defensive Lineman Station

1. Starting Position
   - 4-point stance up on the line of scrimmage
   - see the ball and ignore the quarterback's signals
2. Penetration
   - move when the ball moves
   - do not stand up; stay low
   - keep your head up, and penetrate your gap
   - fight to maintain your position in your zone
   - use your hands to shed a blocker
   - look for the ball carrier
   - wrap, lock and carry to drive the ball carrier back and down
3. Run Penetration Drills

Linebacker Station

1. Starting Position
   - football ready position, hands up and out in front, weight balanced
   - within 3 yards of the line of scrimmage (usually a rule in little kids' football)
   - 6-3 or 5-4 defensive alignment (also, usually a rule)
2. Follow the Ball/Key
   - keep blockers off, using your hands
   - maintain your zone
   - move laterally using the shuffle
   - close your gap quickly; don't wait for runner to come to you
3. Run Pursuit Angle Drills
4. Run Reaction Drills

"THE LINEBACKER AND
THE DEFENSIVE BACK"

Defensive Back Station

1. Starting Position
   - football ready position, hands up and out in front, weight balanced
   - 3 to 5 yards from the line of scrimmage positioned according to defensive alignment
2. Follow the Ball
3. Move Laterally Using Shuffle
4. Retreat
   - move using backward run, avoid turning around
   - keep shoulders and weight over your knees when running backwards
5. Keep Receivers in Front
6. Run Pursuit Angle Drills
7. Run Reaction Drills

Receiver Station

"Three things can happen when you pass, and two of them are bad," said former Ohio State coach Woody Hayes. He didn't like the odds at the college level and would probably like the odds even less in little kids' football. Because the passing game is so difficult for little kids to master, it is better to concentrate on plays the kids can execute and avoid the more advanced maneuvers like long passes until the players get a little older. Therefore, the receiver position station is not stressed at an early age.

Receiver stations, however, can be used to add variety to practice and spice things up for the kids. Little kids love to try to catch passes, but not many can throw the ball very far or very accurately. In our stations, the coach passes the football, and kids learn how to run patterns and how to catch the ball. The completion rate is still quite low, but kids enjoy doing it. The same is true for a passing station with players passing the ball. It's a fun drill to keep the players' interest up, but don't expect John Elway or Dan Marino performance from your 8-year olds.

After exposing the players to position stations, ask them to pick one position on offense and one position on defense they would like to play. Throughout the season, at least in practice and possibly in a game, try to have players spend some time at one of their positions of choice.

"THE FIRST LIVE TACKLING DRILL"

TECHNIQUE DRILLS

Technique drills are for all players to perform throughout the season, regardless of the positions they may be playing. Such practice allows kids to experience more aspects of the game than they might otherwise. It also lets the coach monitor the progress of the players at different positions. For example, the coach may find that a player who was shy during running back stations early in the season is now a tiger when given the ball.

The First Live Tackling Drill

Two players lie on the ground on their backs with their heads about 2 feet apart between two cones that are about 4 feet apart. One of the players is the ball carrier and has the ball. The other is the defender or tackler. When the coach says "go," the two players get to their feet as fast as possible. The runner tries to run through the cones and the defender tries to tackle the runner. The most important thing in this drill is to encourage tacklers to keep their heads up. They have a tendency to lower their heads.

The Four-Corner Drill

This drill is a faster version of the First Live Tackling Drill. It teaches players to get in correct position to make a tackle. Four cones are placed on the ground in a 5-foot square. A runner and a tackler are positioned at adjacent corners of the square. The runner runs diagonally to the opposite cone at half speed. The tackler closes in on the runner on the other diagonal and makes the tackle. Tacklers are

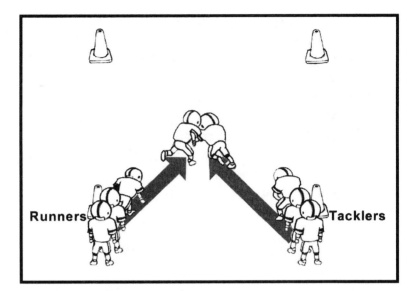

"THE FOUR-CORNER DRILL"

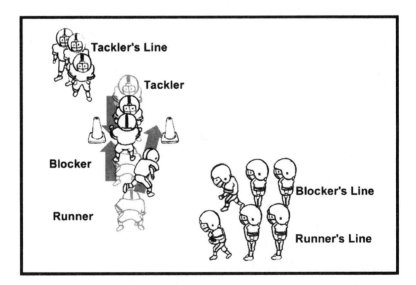

"THE TWO-ON-ONE DRILL"

instructed to make the tackle with their heads up and in front of the runner, not behind him, to avoid arm tackling. Again, encourage tacklers to keep their heads up. Change the lines periodically so that tacklers become runners and runners become tacklers. Also change the position of the tackler from the right side of the runner to the left side of the runner.

The Two-On-One Drill

This drill utilizes a runner, a blocker and a tackler. Two cones are set up about 3 to 4 feet apart to define the running zone for the runner. Blockers take a 3-point stance between the cones and block the would-be tacklers positioned in front of them. The runner, with a ball, lines up 3 yards behind the blocker and, on the coach's start count, runs through the hole opened by the blocker. The coach stands behind the tackler and indicates the start count for the blocker and the runner by means of hand signals and starts the process.

Pursuit Angle Drill

This is a very important drill for newcomers. It is practiced by teams at all levels. It teaches players to maintain defensive position and to follow the proper angles in pursuit of plays across and down field.

Players line up in the formation shown. The coach assumes the quarterback position. The offensive line remains stationary during the drill. The coach calls the snap count, and the defense reacts on the snap. The coach then blows his whistle, and the defense freezes in their positions so the coach can check their alignment. The coach pitches the ball in

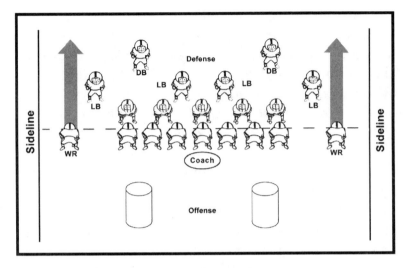

"THE PURSUIT ANGLE DRILL"

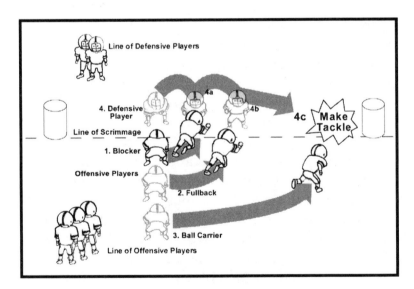

"THE STRING OUT DRILL"

the direction of one of the dummies and yells "swarm." The defensive linemen cover the ball. Instead of pitching the ball back to the dummy, the coach can throw to the wide receiver who runs down the sideline. The defenders pursue, and everyone must touch the receiver with two hands.

The String Out Drill

This drill is used to teach defenders how to string out running plays to the sideline. Players line up in the formation shown. Player #1 is an offensive blocker, player #2 is a blocking back, player #3 is a running back and player #4 is the defensive player. The coach points out the direction of the play to the offensive players who then move on the snap count. Offensive blocker #1 hook blocks the defender at position 4a. The blocking back tries to hook block the defender at position 4b. The running back runs at three-quarter speed around the dummy. The defensive player must play off block #1, block #2 and pursue the ball carrier to make a proper form tackle at position 4c.

The Three-Man Roll

This drill is good for conditioning players and improving their reaction times and coordination. But more important, it is fun and the players like to do it.

Three players line up on all fours with 3 or 4 feet between them. For the purpose of this explanation, the player on the left is #1, the player in the middle is #2, and the player on the right is #3. On "Go," player #1 jumps over player #2, landing on his stomach between #2 and #3. After landing, player #1 then

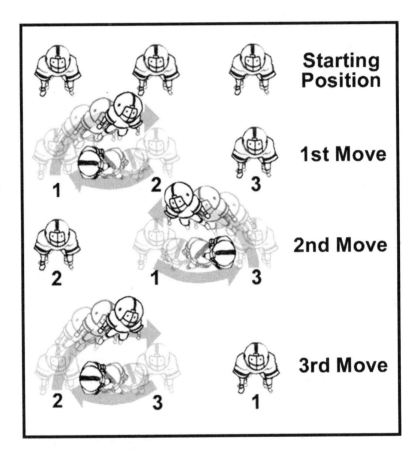

Starting Position

1st Move

2nd Move

3rd Move

"THE THREE-MAN ROLL"

rolls under player #3 who jumps over player #1. Player #3 lands and rolls under player #2 who in turn jumps over player #3. The process is repeated for as long as the players are able to maintain the correct position. I make it a contest in which the team that rolls the longest is excused from a running drill.

Blocking Drill

Blocking is a difficult thing for young kids to master. They have a tendency to grab, hold and tackle. This drill encourages players to fire out on their block, to achieve a good blocking angle and to maintain good balance. Players line up with the blocker facing the "catcher" as shown. The catcher should not try to avoid the block in this drill. In position 1, the catcher lines up in the gap to the right of the blocker. On the snap count, the blocker springs out from his three-point stance, bringing both hands up, engaging the catcher at the bottom of the shoulder pads. The blocker must make his first movement, a short step on the right foot, in the direction of the catcher. The blocker must keep his feet spread in a wide base and use short choppy steps to drive the catcher back.

In position 2, the catcher is to the left of the blocker and the blocker's first step is with the left foot in the direction of the catcher.

In position 3, the blocker must block the catcher to the right or the left, as directed by the coach who stands behind the catcher. If the block is to the left, the blocker's first step must be with the right foot to achieve the best blocking angle. If the block is to the right, the blocker's first step must be with the left foot.

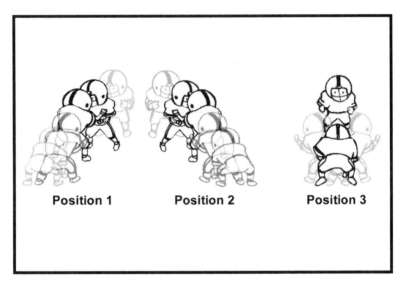

Position 1   Position 2   Position 3

"THE BLOCKER'S DRILL"

Get the Cone Drill

The purpose of this drill is to develop penetration technique by the interior defensive lineman. The defensive lineman is positioned in a 4-point stance in the gap between two offensive blockers. The defensive player must stay low (on all fours if possible) and penetrate the two blockers and reach a cone placed about 2 or 3 yards from the line of scrimmage in the offensive backfield. The coach stands behind the defensive player, indicates a 1, 2 or 3 snap count and then calls signals.

THE PRACTICE PLAN

Practice is the time when coaches really have an influence on their players and can make a big difference in what I call the "fun factor." Practice is the time and place in which players learn to master the skills they will use in the game. It is when they learn their jobs and how to perform them. It is the time they learn to execute the plays they will run in a game. Above all, it is the time when the players gain confidence.

To be effective, practice must be well-organized. It must have goals and objectives, and it must involve and excite all the players, not just the better ones.

It is extremely difficult, if not impossible, for one or two coaches to handle a squad of thirty players during practice. The younger players, especially, require lots of attention. Technique drills are a big part of the teaching process, and small groups are critical for success. Groups of four, five or six ensure each player enough repetitions under a coach's close supervision for the drill to be effective with a minimum number of players standing around waiting for their turn. A 25-player squad should have 4 or 5 coaches, a 35-player squad, at least 6 coaches.

This is where organization and preparation become important. All the coaches need to be on the same page. They must all understand the objectives of the drills, the techniques to be taught and the methods and demonstrations used. Head coaches should prepare a "practice plan" for their assistants and review it with them beforehand.

Many drills are repeated at every practice and become boring for both the players and the coaches.

Boredom is a problem at any age but little kids, especially, get bored easily. A creative coach will add variations to spice up repetitive routines, such as a fumble scramble in the middle of a blocking drill. Keeping player groups small and specific practice situations and individual drills under 20 minutes in duration helps to avoid the tedium.

Technique drills are important for all players and are critical for the less skilled. Through these drills, the supporting cast of blockers, for example, master the movements used to open holes. Some coaches, however, spend an inordinate amount of time running plays in scrimmage at the expense of technique drills and then criticize linemen for missing a block or failing to open a hole. Don't misunderstand; scrimmage time is important for several reasons. As stated earlier, scrimmage is really playing football, much like in a game but better in terms of the kids' enjoyment. It is an essential ingredient to keep practice fun for kids. Scrimmage also is the time the offensive and defensive teams perfect their play execution. But technique drills teach players the fundamentals they need to play their position and are just as vital to successful play execution. They are the foundation upon which a player's self-worth is built. A good practice plan includes both of these important activities.

Coaches that concentrate on improving the execution techniques of their less skilled players will benefit in the long run and more importantly, so will the players. Most youth programs have minimum play rules requiring all players to participate for a certain minimum number of plays in every game.

The team that can substitute players and still maintain a high level of play has a distinct advantage over opponents that cannot.

A Typical Practice Plan

20 minutes—warm-up jog, stretches, calisthenics, running relays and grass drills such as three man rolls and reaction drills
> water break

10 minutes—dummy run—entire team
> water break

15 minutes—blocking drill—four small groups
> water break

15 minutes—tackling drill—four small groups
> water break

5 minutes—fumble drill—four small groups
> water break

15 minutes—two-on-one drill—four small groups
> water break

20 minutes—position stations—five groups
> water break

20 minutes—scrimmage—two half lines then full team
15 minutes—stretch and warm down

A typical early season practice plan is shown. The specific drills have been described. As the season progresses, different drills such as special teams preparation may be added. Frequent water breaks are scheduled, and water should be available at any time to players needing it. This is extremely important during very warm temperatures. Do not, under any circumstances, withhold water from a player as punishment.

One other very important word of caution regarding practice. At the very first practice, even before equipment is distributed, the coach must make a mandatory rule concerning football helmets. The coach must remind the players about the rule once helmets are distributed. The rule is that ALL PLAYERS ARE REQUIRED TO WEAR HELMETS AS SOON AS THEY STEP ON THE PRACTICE FIELD. HELMETS SHALL NOT BE REMOVED UNLESS DIRECTED BY THE COACH. No player should be allowed on the practice field without his helmet on and strapped up. This rule is for the protection of the players. If some players have their helmets on and others do not, the ones without helmets are in jeopardy. A collision between a player wearing a helmet and one without a helmet can be dangerous.

Injuries can occur in the few minutes before a scheduled practice starts. Players may arrive at the field early. Some drop their helmets off to the side. These early birds often begin running, chasing and tackling each other, some with helmets and some without. The coach must impress on his players how dangerous this activity can be. The mandatory helmet rule must be followed whenever players are on the practice field, even if practice has not started.

Helmets seem heavy and somewhat uncomfortable until players get used to them. The coach should allow all players to remove helmets during water breaks or other lulls in practice. Make sure the kids know when the break period is over, and helmets must go back on. Don't start any activity until all players are properly equipped.

"GIVE US FIVE, COACH!"

DISCIPLINE CAN BE FUN, TOO

If you've ever watched a little kids' football game, it's easy to recognize an undisciplined team. They have trouble getting into and out of the huddle and up to the line of scrimmage properly. Players wander around out of position and jump offside regularly. So even though football is fun to play and is not difficult for kids to learn, it takes a fair amount of discipline for them to play well and avoid unnecessary penalties and mistakes. The discipline referred to here is the discipline to pay attention, to listen and to remember.

Offensive players must remember the play, the formation, the snap count and the object of their block. The players must get into and out of the huddle quickly without help. They must learn to be quiet and pay attention to the quarterback in the huddle. They must all line up in the correct formation. Defensive players must remember their zones and learn to watch the ball to avoid jumping offside. For 7- and 8-year-old kids, with short attention spans these objectives present a challenge that the coach must work on from the very first day of practice. Cadence drills are effective in introducing this type of discipline to young kids.

Cadence drills are simply commands that the coach gives the team to execute a simple instruction on a specific count or number. For example, the coach will say, "Let's have a two clap on two! . . . Hut 1 . . . Hut 2" and the team responds with two claps. The next time the claps will be on three or on one and so on. We do this kind of cadence drill continuously for

5 minutes during our opening exercises. The kids like it and it gets them into the habit of listening for and executing commands together. It can also be used as a fun competition between units to see which one can perform the longest without making a mistake. The usual penalty for an infraction is five push-ups. Sometimes even the coach makes a mistake, and the kids love it when a coach has to do five push-ups.

To reinforce the habit of remembering the snap count, every drill we do at practice that is initiated by a start number is run on two or three at the start of the season. We also run all our plays during scrimmages at the start of the season on snap counts other than one. The kids learn quickly to pay attention to the numbered command in whatever form they hear it.

Since defensive players move on ball movement, not snap count, we have ball movement drills. These drills involve intentional signal calling in combination with ball movement. The defense reacts only on the ball movement. If the ball doesn't move, the defense cannot move.

Time spent in early season practice instilling good habits is time extremely well spent. Use huddle drills to teach players how to get in and out of the huddle quickly. Conduct drills that teach the offense or the defense to run on and off the field quickly. Create special teams drills to get the special team players on the field and in the proper positions. A drill to teach the kids how to line up for calisthenics is an absolute necessity. It's strange, but 25 kids can have a major problem getting themselves into five lines with five players in each line. They need to learn how to do it, or you will spend 20 minutes of every practice getting the players lined up properly.

If there is something we want the kids to learn to do together, we'll create a fun drill for it, usually involving a competition of sorts. We are really teaching discipline in an enjoyable way.

"THE RACE IS ON"

CONDITIONING

Proper conditioning can improve a player's performance and reduce the risk of injury. It is an essential part of practice but one that players usually don't like. The phase of practice dedicated solely to conditioning takes about 20 minutes and typically includes a warm-up exercise, usually slow a jog around the field; followed by a period of stretching for each of the major muscles groups; followed by several different calisthenics, including push-ups, sit-ups, leg lifts and jumping-jacks; and finally, grass drills; runs and sprints.

The conditioning period does not have to be drudgery or a totally unpleasant experience for the players, although doing calisthenics is what most kids like least. So it is important to keep these exercises to the minimum necessary. Also try to integrate some of these things into other drills, or make contests or competitions out of them. For example, a relay race that includes a dummy carry and a five-count push-up or sit-up station can turn wind sprints and calisthenics into an exciting activity. Also kids enjoy running backwards so consider a backwards race as a part of your conditioning regimen.

Players should have the opportunity to cool down and stretch again at the conclusion of practice.

EVERYBODY PLAYS

Any youth football program that is worth its while has some requirement that ensures playing time for all players. Pop Warner football has a mandatory play rule. The rule stipulates that every player on the roster must play in some minimum number of plays depending upon the size of the roster. For teams with 16-25 players on the roster, the minimum is eight plays. For teams with 26-35 players, the minimum is six plays. Our intramural program that had roster sizes of between 16-18 players required that every player play in at least one half of the game.

Little kids' football games are usually comprised of four 10-minute quarters, but the clock runs almost continuously because there is so little passing. As a result, the game goes by very quickly. Typically, there may be 30 offensive plays and 30 defensive plays per team in a game, if the teams are evenly matched. Considering that there are about 60 possible plays in a game, a minimum play rule of 6 or 8 plays for each player is really not very many.

Some leagues, like Pop Warner, prohibit players at the youngest age level from playing offense and defense in the same half. This means that the maximum number of possible plays for offensive players might only be 30. Again six to eight plays are not very many. Such limited playing time does not really constitute the full and fair measure of play that was discussed earlier.

Regardless of the minimum play rule requirements, in the heat of the game coaches often forget about making substitutions unless they have been well-thought-out before hand. To get all players into the game and to ensure adequate playing time for everyone requires planning and control. It is best to assign one coach the responsibility of putting players in and out of the game according to a pregame plan.

The coach should plan to have each player play in at least half of the possible plays in a game. The best substitution strategy is to make sure that every player has satisfied the minimum play requirement by the end of the first half of the game. Then the coach can use the second half to increase the playing time of players that are substitutes.

Basically, our first unit plays the first quarter or until their minimum play requirement has been met. The second unit then comes in and plays the second quarter or until their minimum requirement has been met. In the second half we follow the same pattern but adjust the substitutions so that players that played fewer plays in the first half get to play more plays in the second half. With planning and a coach assigned to implement the plan, it is not difficult follow this strategy, even with 35 players on the team. The substitution plan should be followed without regard for the score. Player participation must take precedence over winning the game.

THE PLAYER WHO IS OUT OF PLACE

Occasionally, the coach finds a player on his team who is completely out of place—one who isn't able to perform the simplest drills and exercises or cannot follow directions or concentrate for more than a few seconds. The player is clearly unhappy and shouldn't be playing football. The player may be too young or immature, either physically or emotionally. Or the player may simply be a child who does not enjoy football's rough-and-tumble activity.

If this happens, the coach should bring the situation to attention of the player's parents and recommend they do what is best for the child and take the youngster off the team. Kids who do not want to play or are not capable of playing and enjoying the game should not be forced. Leaving the player on the team is not fair to the player, the coach or the other team members. In a year or two, the player may be more ready or interested in playing.

To my best recollection, this situation occurred just once in all my years as a coach and as it turned out, the player returned to play and have fun two seasons later.

THE COACH WHO IS OUT OF PLACE

Sometimes it is the coach and not the player who is out of place. Here's another short quiz prepared especially for youth coaches. Parents can also use this quiz to evaluate a coach or to better understand the mentality necessary to be a good youth coach. Coaches should use this quiz as a check list to ensure they don't lose sight of the priorities of kids' sports programs.

Coaches' Quiz

1. Do you think kids need to win to have fun in a competitive sport?

☐ Yes ☐ No

2. Have you ever had an argument with a game official in a kids' sport?

☐ Yes ☐ No

3. Do you endorse Vince Lombardi's remark that "Winning isn't everything, it's the only thing" when it comes to kids' sports?

☐ Yes ☐ No

4. As a coach, have you ever bent the rules to improve your team's chances to win.?

☐ Yes ☐ No

5. Do you think the better players on a team should get more playing time than the ones who aren't as good?

☐ Yes ☐ No

6. Do you spend more time working with the better kids at practice?

☐ Yes   ☐ No

7. As a coach have you raised your voice in anger at a player for making a mistake or an error?

☐ Yes   ☐ No

8. If a team you coached never won a game during the season, would you blame the players?

☐ Yes   ☐ No

9. If a team you coached never won a game during the seasonm would you feel they let you down?

☐ Yes   ☐ No

10. Do you put substitute players in a game only when your team is either far ahead or far behind but not when the game is close?

☐ Yes   ☐ No

You may have guessed that the "correct" answer to all of these questions for a good youth coach should be no. The coach who answers yes to all ten of the above questions is too intensely focused on winning and probably should seek employment with a professional sports team. Certainly, the individual should not be coaching young children.

PARENTAL INVOLVEMENT

Over the years, parental involvement has gone from totally non-existent to almost total involvement. When I was young, adults were never a part of our "unorganized" athletic activities. In the generation following mine, parents got involved as coaches and spectators as well as organizers of the sports programs for kids. Leagues for organized athletic competition sprouted up everywhere with Mom or Dad or both in key positions of leadership or administration. Not surprisingly, this parental involvement usually stops when the child or children stop playing.

As a result, most of the youth coaches of any sport today are parents of children who are playing. New children usually mean new parents and new coaches. Since I am an old coach coaching a young group, most of the players and parents on my teams are newcomers to the program. I make it a point before the start of the season to meet with the parents for an hour or so and talk about the program and its objectives, my philosophy, our coaches, player weight requirements, equipment requirements, practice and game schedules or other important dates, special playing rules, practice descriptions, homework priorities, missed practices, individual playing time, in-season communications, meal scheduling, special player or parental needs or hardships, emergency procedures, transportation needs and parental expectations and involvement. This meeting is the first step in building positive parental support of the team and the coaches.

An important fact for coaches to keep in mind is that in many families today, both parents work. Over 76% of the moms today work outside the home and 25% of families are single-female-parent families. This means that getting kids to practice on time can often be a significant hardship. The coach can ease the problem in several ways. First, by holding practice at the same time and on the same day(s) of the week so that routines can be established. It will be easier for the player and the parent to remember. Many times when kids miss practice it is because it was not convenient or possible for a parent to provide transportation. Car pools are a big help and the coach should take a key role in helping to set them up. Make sure each parent has a team roster containing the addresses and phone numbers of all players and coaches. As a last resort, I tell all my players to call me if they ever need a ride to practice or to a game. While I'm on the subject of rides, it should go without saying that a youth coach should never leave practice until all players on the team have been picked up.

After the parents' meeting, I also have a separate meeting with all coaches to discuss coaching philosophy, team building, fun building, practice plans, position stations and drills, exercises and calisthenics, playing rules, coaches assignments, plays and play books and the coach's code of conduct. This way we will all start off on the same page and heading for the same objectives. It is a good idea to get together with all the coaches periodically during the season to make adjustments in practice plans, review players' progress or discuss assigning players to different positions.

It is important that coaches and parents both understand, up front, the extent to which each will be involved with the team during the season. Things will always come up later but by having these two basic start-up meetings you can avoid a great deal of initial confusion, inconvenience and the possible bad feelings that may result.

PARENTS' CODE OF CONDUCT

There have been several articles and a few books written advising the parents of children who participate in youth sports programs. For the most part the advice is simple and straight forward. The key elements are summarized below:

- Be interested but not overbearing about your child's participation.
- Be a good listener when your child wants to talk about his experience.
- Don't put pressure on your child to win or excel. Help to keep the child's focus on fun and participation.
- Avoid over-reacting to wins or losses.
- Provide positive reinforcement for the player and the team.
- Take part in your team's special events and activities.
- Understand what the coach is trying to teach your child so that you can be in a position to reinforce the coach's instruction at home.
- Avoid coaching your player from the sidelines at games or in practices; stick to words of encouragement.
- Check with the coach if you have suggestions you think may benefit your child. Don't send the player to practice with a message for the coach saying "my Dad says I should do it this way."
- Since you may well be acting as a "coach at

home" try to follow the suggestions made earlier about coaching little kids. Keep things simple, criticize the technique not the player and balance criticism with praise.

- Inform the coach if your child is having problems, either with practices or with school work or if your child must miss a practice or a game.

- Do your part to ensure a drug, alcohol and tobacco free environment at youth sports events

- Keep your emotions under control, especially during games. Remember, these are little kids playing a game for fun.

- Never put down, deride or disparage your child's opponents, they are little kids too. Root *for* your team, not *against* the opponents.

- Review the coaches' code of conduct. Expect and require your child's coach to abide by that code. Where appropriate substitute the word parent for coach and follow that lead.

Here again, the National Alliance for Youth Sports provides valuable information and guidance. Their division known as the **Parents' Association for Youth Sports (PAYS)** has prepared a Parent's Code of Ethics that every sport parent should read and endorse. It is re-printed, as Appendix B, with their permission.

"FROM THE SIDELINES"

About 5 years ago I developed a weekly team newsletter called "From The Sidelines" to provide a formal line of communication among coaches, players and parents throughout the season. "From The Sidelines" contains detailed information concerning the practice schedule and changes to it, practice progress, a word about our upcoming game, its time and place, directions to away fields, players' development and any other important information parents might need or want to know. Of course, some of this information is announced to players following practice, but most kids aren't known for their accuracy and reliability in conveying messages.

In addition, the newsletter is a perfect vehicle to provide positive feedback and recognition to the team, to individual units and to individual players. It also gives me another opportunity to say things that help take the sting out of a tough loss or to keep winning and losing in perspective.

"From The Sidelines" recaps the positive highlights of the previous week's game and provides offensive and defensive statistics such as yards gained by the team and by individuals, tackles made by the top tacklers, key blocks by offensive linemen, fumble recoveries, interceptions or other outstanding plays. It is a great opportunity to praise players who have worked especially hard either in the game or during practice. I have found over the years that sometime during the season, every player on the team will find his name highlighted in the newsletter, at least once, for something special he did the past week. It is not necessary to try to do this; it just happens. Every player on the team will do something worthy of note sometime during the season. The coach just needs to pay attention and jot it down when it happens. Needless to say, the parents and the players both look forward to the Tuesday practice when "From The Sidelines" is distributed.

With the increased availability of home computers and the Internet, "From The Sidelines" could easily be distributed electronically via a web site or e-mail.

Two issues of "From the Sidelines" are included as an example for coaches to follow. Players last names have been edited out to protect the individual's privacy.

PONTE VERDA BEACH- MIGHTY MITES

FROM THE SIDELINES

September 1997,   *Vol 7*

Panthers 7-Grand Park 6

The Panthers played another excellent as well as exciting game against Grand Park. Our Mighty Mites were the only Ponte Vedra team that won at Grand Park, which says something about their program. If you were at the game, you saw that Grand Park has a well-established program that includes a flag football program for their little guys and girls. Their flag program really helps prepare the young players for the tackle game. The Mighty Mite Cardinals were a good team and were very well disciplined although not as fast as some of our other opponents.

Grand Park's only touchdown came on a terrific pass

play that little kids just are not expected to make. It is probably a play their kids learned and worked on in their flag program. It certainly took us by surprise. But our guys responded very well. They didn't get down after that play. Instead, they got fired up and made probably the biggest play of the game for us when they stopped the extra point attempt. That play gave us the opportunity to win the ball game with a touchdown and extra point.

We really dominated the game despite being down 6-0 until the fourth quarter. For example, we controlled the ball for 48 plays compared to 24 plays by Grand Park. We gained over 175 yards rushing compared to just 90 yards by the Cardinals (not including the 75 yards they gained on the touchdown pass). After we kicked off to the Cardinals to start the second half, they ran four plays and our defense held them to a minus 5 yards. We took over and ran 20 plays in a row and marched down the field for the tying touchdown. In that sequence we gained 60 yards and made four first downs. Other than one penalty against us for a false start, we gained yardage on every play we ran. It was a magnificent drive and used up the entire third quarter and half of the fourth quarter. There was a very big play in that drive that may have gone unnoticed. We were at the Cardinal 35 yard line and had a fourth down and 4 yards to go for a first down. We made it and the drive for the touchdown continued!

What a great job of blocking by the entire offense. The backside blocking was our best to date. Bobby, Kevin, Mikey, Michael and Kody did a great job. Tyler, John and Cole on the strong side were simply awesome. What it came down to is that we won the game because we scored the extra point and the Cardinals didn't, and we scored the winning point because Blake made a terrific block on the Grand Park defensive end enabling Andrew to get into the end zone.

Our defense played probably their best game to date. There were so many gang tackles that it is difficult to get an accurate count for our "tackles made" statistics. Joe provided the penetration we have been looking for by the defensive line. Evan and Christopher did another great job stopping the sweep, and what can I say about the play of our two cornerbacks Cory and Patrick? Patrick had a marvelous pass interception, and Cory also had an interception that for some unexplained reason was not allowed by the officials. They both made tackles all over the field.

Statistical Highlights: Andrew ran for 163 yards. Arin, Cory and Heath led the defense in tackles with four each. PJ and Joe were next with three. Tyler got credit for a pancake block on the kickoff following the Grand Park touchdown.

Practice Schedule: Practice this week as usual, Tuesday at 5:30 pm at Cornerstone Park, Thursday at 5:30 pm at the practice field and a walk-through (helmets and game jerseys—no pads) on Friday from 5:30 to 6:30 pm at Cornerstone Park.

Our Next Game: This week's game is Saturday, October 4 at home against the North Quadrant Bumble Bees at 8 am. This is a very early start so make sure your player gets to bed early and gets up early. Be at the Cornerstone Park field at 7:00 am.

Talk to you next week—Jerry Norton

PONTE VERDA BEACH- MIGHTY MITES

FROM THE SIDELINES

September 1998,   *Vol 5*

Saturday's Game
North Jax 7 - Ponte Vedra Panthers 6

If you were there, I don't need to describe how exciting the game was and how well the Panthers played. If you weren't there, I'm not sure I can do it justice. What I can say is if you watch football games for the rest of your life, little kids', high school, college or the pros, you will never see a more exciting ending to a game than happened on Saturday. The score was 7-6 in favor of North Jax with only a minute left to play and North Jax had the ball. The Panther defense stopped the Jaguars on a fourth down play, and we got the ball back with less than 30 seconds left in the game. We had the ball on our own 3 yard line and with enough time for only one or at most 2 plays left, quarterback Drew handed off to Taylor, who rolled to his left and back into the end zone. Zach, our left end, and left tackle Larson gave Taylor key blocks that sprung him to the outside. He avoided several tacklers at the 5 yard line and again at the 15 and then sprinted down the sidelines 104 yards for a touchdown! It was the game-winning TD. It was, that is, until the referee called the play back on a penalty against the Panthers. From euphoria to despair! But not for our guys; they never quit. There was still time for one more play. This time Drew handed to Michael who ran to the right behind blocks by Taylor, Mike H. and Matt. Michael ran for almost 70 yards before he was knocked out-of-bounds to end the game. I was very, very proud of the boys. It was disappointing for them, of course, but I think they understood that, more important than the outcome of the game, they all played hard right through to the very last play. They never gave up. They certainly had played well enough to win. The referee's call can take away the winning touchdown, but it cannot erase that accomplishment in the minds of the players. I believe Taylor will remember that touchdown forever. The boys could all hold their heads high after the game and feel very good about how they played. They were clearly the better team on Saturday. They were simply terrific.

Statistics: The Panthers gained 170 yards compared to 114 for North Jax. Michael picked up 122 yards on eight carries and Taylor 25 yards on eight carries, not counting the 104 yard touchdown run that was called back. Our defense made the big plays when they had to, and we had 11 different guys make tackles this week. Blake led with eight tackles, Matt had seven and Devin and Zach had five each. Zach also recovered a fumble. I was especially pleased with the way Kyle and Ross played in the defensive secondary.

Help Wanted-Still:

We are still in need of a parent who has a video camcorder and will take videos of the games for us. We did this last year, and it was a big help for the coaches and the players in making adjustments to the offense and defense. We also made a composite video of all our games last year and gave copies to each player as a memento. Please contact me if you could do this very important job.

Practice This Week:

Tuesday 5:30 to 7:30 pm at practice field—PGA Tour parking lot

Thursday 5:30 to 7:30 pm at Cornerstone Park game field.

Next Week's Game:

We play the Lake Shore Ramblers at Lake Shore, Saturday, September 12 at 10 am. We must be there by 9 am for the weigh-in. We will assemble at the Fresh Market parking lot at 8 am and depart for Lake Shore no later than 8:15 am.

Talk to you next week—Jerry Norton

THE POSTGAME WRAP-UP

A COACH FOR ALL SEASONS

I t should be obvious by now that these discussions about coaching young children really apply to all organized youth sports. It doesn't make any difference whether you are coaching little kids' football or little kids' baseball, little kids' tennis or little kids' soccer, the principles and fundamentals of fun and participation are transferable and interchangeable. Your priorities, as a coach, should be the same. Number one priority is player safety, number two is fun and number three is learning or player development. The rules of the game may be different. The position station drills and the technique drills that are used may be different. But the top three priorities must remain.

The challenge for youth coaches, whatever the sport, is to keep their desire to win from displacing one of these top three priorities. I was watching a baseball game recently involving 8- and 9-year-old players. A batter came to the plate with no one on base and his coach, after getting the boy to step out of the batters' box, flashed a series of signs which the youngster studied intently. The batter then took five or six pitches, some which were very close to the strike zone, and drew a base on balls without making any effort to swing the bat. It was quite obvious that the coach had instructed the batter not to swing. It was more important to this coach to have a base runner than for the player to have an opportunity to try to hit the ball. In this case the coach's desire to win took precedence over the player's development and probably his enjoyment of the game.

When a coach's desire to win displaces one of the three priorities, the priority most in jeopardy is "Fun." All too often, coaches compromise a player's opportunity to have fun by denying playing time to a less-accomplished player in favor of a better player. In many cases, the rules of the youth organization may even permit this. For example, many youth baseball programs require that a player bat at least once and play some minimum number of innings in the field during a game. In this situation, there are coaches who will "play by the rules" and take out a poor hitter after just one at-bat and substitute a better hitter for the rest of the game. Doesn't the poor hitter deserve to have as much fun as the better hitter? He does if the priority is fun. A better rule in this situation is to allow all players on the team to bat in order whether they are playing in the field or not. This alternative has worked very well in the youth league in my community.

Winning becomes more and more of a priority as young athletes advance in age and skill level. With advancement, competition increases and playing time is the reward for the better player. Winning is the justification. In professional sports, winning is the bottom line. This situation will come all too soon for young players as they grow up. In fact, in most high school sports, winning is a high priority.

But remember, nearly 70% of the youngsters who participate in organized youth sports drop out of participation before they are 13. The top reasons are: not playing, abusive coaches and an overemphasis on winning. Clearly, for these drop-outs, fun, the number two priority, was replaced by someone else's desire to win.

POEMS FROM THE PAST

One of the highlights of every football season, for the players and their parents and also for me, comes at the end of the year in the form of a humorous poem about our team. I start thinking about the team poem on the first day of practice and store things away, throughout the season, that are funny or memorable. Every player is mentioned at some point in the poem, always in a positive or lighthearted manner. I read the poem at an end-of-the-year party at which all players are individually recognized for their participation and their contribution to the team. This tradition started many years ago when my own kids played and I have done it for every team since then. This collection of poems is priceless to me. It contains a lifetime of wonderful memories.

This final chapter contains just a few of these team poems, some reproduced in their entirety as well as excerpts from several others. I have changed the last names of the players and coaches to protect their privacy. These poems help to convey the message that little kids' football can be a wonderful experience for the player, the parents and the coach. I hope you will use these poems as templates or as the framework for poems about your own team. Substitute the names of your players, your team and your town, where appropriate. Try to keep the rhyme and the meter intact. It's fun and the kids will enjoy the result.

THE BIRTH OF THE PANTHERS

When the talk is of football along the First Coast
It isn't the Jaguars who are talked about most.
It's those boys from the beach, Ponte Vedra, I mean
The Mighty Mite Panthers, America's team

A thought, an idea, plus the work of a few
Took a dream to play football and made it come true.
So the Panthers were born in the very same year
As Jacksonville's Jaguars. I'm glad they're both here.

Our very first practice was August the first.
A day when a camel could work up a thirst.
We'd not even started — just lined up I think
When Joshua James asked "Can I get a drink?"

"Me too" in the form of an echo did ring,
Delaying the fun calisthenics would bring.
Like push-ups and wind sprints and stretches galore.
Then hearing coach Tim ask "Who wants to do more?"

Before you could block, make a tackle or kick,
Conditioning needed — you could then take a lick.
The key to conditioning as I recall
Was making it fun without using a ball.

Those first weeks, a difficult, challenging time.
Some might think it easy to form a straight line!
The concepts we used left some players perplexed,
Like counting to three — after two what comes next?

And strange football jargon like "Please take a knee."
It's amazing how vague that instruction can be.
When stated like that, who knows what should be done?
We must be specific and tell them which one.

Equipment arrived—it would have to fit right
Is your mouthpiece attached? Are your shoulder pads tight?
The size of the pants went from huge down to small.
The huge would fit David, not Bobby or Paul.

Our helmets adjustable, filled up with air.
One size might fit all if inflated with care.
"That helmet's too big, try a small one instead
And if that doesn't work we'll just pump up your head!"

In running a team there is much to be done.
So we asked a few mothers to join in the fun.
Those Mighty Mite Moms what an organized crew.
They make our lives easy, like Moms always do.

At last we were ready, equipment all fit.
Now we'd find who could run and we'd find who could hit.
You'd learn how to huddle, what stance you should take.
You'd learn how a back makes a hand off or fake.

The coaches would help you get ready to play
So listen and hear what they each have to say.
Coach Seaver, Laruso, Del Weaver and Tom
And also Coach Robins, a coach and a Mom.

In football you have to remember so much,
Like snap counts and spacings, when's practice and such.
And numerous plays, the formations, the set.
You need a good memory, there's much to forget.

Joe Daily, all dressed up and ready to play?
He came without pants to our practice one day.
"He what?" said Jake Seaver on hearing the news.
Then Jake came to practice forgetting his shoes

We numbered the holes and the backs for our plays.
Then practiced and practiced and practiced for days.
The T or the I or the shot-gun employed.
The fumbles of course we would need to avoid.

For offense, some linemen to make up a wall,
Like someone humongous, say twenty feet tall.
And runners so quick, they'd have wings on their feet
Would sure make the Panthers a tough team to beat.

We searched for some guys we could count on to block.
Two guys come to mind and they both are named Strock.
We'll try Warren Matthews, let's see what he'll do.
And Robins and Jeffro, Ty Halliday too.

To fill up the backfield, the problem was small,
Four runners, but no one to give them the ball.
We'll open with Andrew and finish with Bogg.
They make it look easy, like falls from a log.

For ends we'll try Cory or Bradley or Matt
To block on the corners and knock 'em down flat.
Our fullback a blocker named Alexandro.
We'll fake it to him and watch Jonathan go.

The offensive coach had the easiest task.
Just call the right plays, Matt, that's all that I ask.
And which are the right ones? I'm sure you will find
It's simply a matter of reading my mind!

And now for the defensive side of the ball,
Which accounts for the gray in the hair of coach Paul.
Success for the defense, so much would depend
On the play of the tackle and defensive end.

Selecting our ends would take one or two games,
There's Mitchell and Jake also Christopher Raymes.
One tackle a giant name Jared Millroy,
The other assignment to Doc Barren's boy.

The strength of our defense, our linebacking crew.
There's Bubba and Stevo to name only two.
Plus PJ and CJ, Bob, Billy and Blake
And Hunter. Now how many guys does that make?

It makes twenty-eight if my numbers are right
And it's those twenty-eight whom we honor tonight.
A team for all seasons, the first of a line
And one I'll remember a very long time.

You're special not only because you're the first.
As players, collectively far from the worst.
You're really quite good, that our scores do attest.
In terms of improvement, I'm sure you're the best.

No matter the place or position you played
Important is what contribution you made.
On offense or defense, a lineman or back,
A block's just as big as a quarterback sack!

Look back on the season and each of the games.
The Colts and the Cowboys were some of the names.
No matter the outcome, whatever the score,
You all did your best, I could ask nothing more.

Yes look back with pride at the way you all played,
At the distance you came and the progress you made.
A wonderful season, a fantastic year!
Now let's close for tonight with that loud Panther cheer.

circa 1995

THE JAGUARS OR THE PANTHERS?

In Florida, football's the number one game
The Noles and the Gators two teams you could name
And also the Jaguars—our pride and our joy.
Each player's an idol for every young boy.

Especially these Panthers just learning to play.
This Mighty Mite team that we honor today.
A look at the lineups I think would be fun
The Jags or the Panthers and who's number one!

Their quarterback's good—he's a fellow named Mark
But not like that kid out at Cornerstone Park.
Our Matt's got his moves and much more, if you please.
He also has two perfect undamaged knees.

Their offensive line's got some really big men
Rich Tylski, Boselli, could block now and then
But can they compare to our Mighty Mite crew
Of Ian and Morton, Ty Halliday, too?

We also had Willis whose 56 pounds
Is muscle and brains—as strange as that sounds
And what about Joshua Cleary and Bloch
They made some big plays and they hit like a rock!

Widell, the Jags center, is big and he's fat
Our guy on the Panthers looks nothing like that.
He's tall and he's tough and he's hard as a rock
He's much better looking, and Chandler can block!

The backs for the Jaguars, not bad, I recall
James Stewart and Natrone could carry the ball.
But not like the Panther who wears 22.
His name isn't Andy. Please call him An-drew!

And don't forget Blake, who could throw, kick and run
Or play well on D if we needed someone.
At flanker, the Jaguars' McCardell could fly.
But he's not as fast as this Nickovich guy.

Pete Mitchell the Jaguar who plays the tight end
Could stop any blitz that the defense might send.
He does what he can, but I'll say it again
"There's no one can do, what Cole 'Do a Lot' can!"

At offensive end, we've a short and a tall
Who never expect us to throw them the ball!
The tall one is Mike and be sure to include
The one who's named Kody, our own surfer dude.

The Jaguars on defense, some very big names
But so do the Panthers—We've Christopher Raymes
The Jaguars have Smeenge, and Pritchard, that's true
But oh! what O'Malley and Doty can do.

Laruso and Brody, and Evan and Heath
Would hit you so hard you might lose a few teeth!
If they didn't get you, you better look out
Cause Patrick and Cory are coming, no doubt!

That man in the middle? Young Alex O'Shea
Just super! He's sure to be famous some day.
And Mikey, though many may think he's too small,
He plays like he's fifteen or twenty feet tall.

And Topper, the Hopper thinks hitting is fun.
I wonder if Kevin could teach him to run?
Another tough Panther, the guy they call Nate
It's Nathan—but I call him Nater the Great!

And don't forget Billy, he played a key role
He'd clog up the middle. Chris called him the Mole.
His lifetime ambition?—to run with the ball.
He'll learn all the plays and then do it next fall.

Well now that I'm finished, it should be quite clear!
You Panthers are really the team of the year!
Your season is over. I hope it's been fun.
Please tell me together now, Who's number one?

circa 1997

THE MICE

"Twas the middle of August and down at the Y
Hundreds of boys would give football a try.
Some big ones, some small ones, some naughty, some nice
All with but one hope . . . making the Mice.

They came with their cleats and with fancy new shirts,
They left in the evening all dirty with hurts.
They came weighing fifty and strange as it sounds,
They came weighing one hundred twenty-three pounds.

Alas there's a limit in age and in size
The weigh-in at Brentwood brought tears to some eyes.
The eighty pound weight meant for some boys a diet.
If you made it, some ice cream, the coaches would buy it.

The days went along and more practices showed
That we had a few guys who knew how to unload.
Roy Mellinger charged with a fire in his eyes.
Lex Baker could block someone three times his size.

Bonacki, a linebacker, knew how to hit
Though he walks like a guy who has shoes that don't fit.
And Ed as a linemen could sure lead a play.
That is if he felt like trying that day.

The Mice had a runner who'll go on to fame.
James Whaley, James Whaley, remember that name.
And David McCue, all the moves of a pro.
Just fake it to Whaley and watch David go.

We practiced each weekend and during the week
We practiced the ride and the quarterback sneak.
We practiced with Harper and Mike Catapino
If we practice much more, my wife's going to Reno!

We practiced in sunshine but never in rain
Nor thunder and lightning—so lost a big game.
The Boy's Club they beat us. A very close score.
To the rest of the league we would lose not one more.

You boys all worked harder the next several days
And showed them from Brookhaven that good practice pays.
John Reardon and Parkinson came along fine
And Brentwood was beaten by our defensive line.

Well that is our team—look on them with pride
As coach it's an honor to be on their side.
Our team is the best at the YMCA
I'm sure it's the best in the whole USA.

circa 1968

THE RAIDERS

Football fans from New York, have you suffered enough?
The Jets are rebuilding—The Giants aren't tough.
If it's football you want that's exciting to see
Then the Raiders my choice. Why? Just listen to me.

The Jets' big attraction, Joe Namath could throw.
But if called on to run he was pitifully slow.
Our quarterback ran—"Keeper Right" he would beg.
He's faster than Joe when he taped up his leg.

Sure the Giants have Czonka—Three million he cost
But still as a team they've done nothing but lost.
Our fullback's the key to our running attack.
Chris'll carry six guys twenty yards on his back!

To round out our backfield, the best one around
There's Jessie and Neil—they can cover some ground.
Opponents bewildered, which one had the ball?
The outcome was certain—A touchdown, that's all.

Though the backfield was good, they'd need someone to block
A collection of guys who could rock and could sock!
The line we assembled to help move the ball
Would make both the Giants and Jets team look small.

Our tackles, two monsters called Michael and Pete
With long hairy arms and size twenty feet.
When they moved off the ball, why the ground even shook.
There were times in some games, I was too scared to look.

Next the guards, somewhat shorter but tougher than nails.
What opponents were facing were two killer whales.
If Dennis and Chris blocked a hole in a wall
It'd be six feet across—just a yard or so tall.

At center two things I was sure we would need.
One—get the ball back and I mean at top speed
And then after the snap make a block on the play.
I knew Bill could do it that very first day.

One problem resolved by a very neat trick
Was where to play Johnny, Bill, Robert and Rick?
At the ends! What a ploy, how deceptive and sly
They'd miss them out there if the grass got too high.

This offense—no fear—we were certain to score.
The question was now "Would opponents score more?"
In our very first game it all became clear
From our defensive line we had nothing to fear.

We'd play a six three, the defensive ends box
Then tackle those runners right out of their socks.
If in sheer desperation, to a pass, they'd resort
In this critical spot is Matt really too short?

The answer of course is emphatically not.
If they threw it his way he would stretch quite a lot.
That explains how he picked off a pass meant for Mise,
An end that I swear must be three times his size.

Our defense fantastic. Our ends were superb.
To consider a sweep was completely absurd.
The middle was closed every play I recall
By Chris, Neil or Michael or Dennis or Paul.

As a team you're the best. You have really come far.
For the job you all did you should all get a star.
And it's not just because of the games that you won,
But the effort you made to improve and have fun.

That's really the reason you came here to play,
With this team in St. Pats. It's been fun I can say.
For the rest of the year all your voices can rest.
Now I'll ask one last time, as a team "Who's the Best?"

circa 1972

ST. PATRICKS FOOTBALL

From seasons long past, football stories are told
Of players and coaches now long since grown old.
Lombardi and Landry are names you all know.
Dick Butkis, Unitas, the Jet Broadway Joe.

They'll soon be replaced by some folks gathered here
From the things that I saw down at Mill Dam this year.
Let's look at each team and recall for today,
Some names, some events or some really big play.

I'll start with the Little Guys, eager and green.
The football they played was the strangest I've seen.
Our very first game, someone wanted to know
"Mr. Norton, how many more innings to go?"

The first several weeks there was much to recall.
"Was offense or defense the one with the ball?"
A flanker, a notch back, a split end or tight.
Please try to remember your left from your right.

A few simple plays at the start were enough.
Just to center the ball to the quarterback's tough.
Now break from the huddle, now "Ready" now "Set"
If we don't run on one someone's sure to forget.

With practice and patience your skills did improve.
The defense grew tough, soon the offense could move.
We changed up the backfield, we mixed up the line
A new team each week I would try to define.

The Blue might have Warren, Scott, Nicky or Dean
Or Joey the Giant, ferocious and mean.
The Merrells or Meister or Tom I might choose
To play with John Callee and Eddie White Shoes.

Next week maybe Joshua, Rico or Ted
Would team up with Barry and Eric the Red.
Or Billy and David, Todd, Kevin and Shane
With Noel and Anthony—matchups remain.

No matter the teams, pure excitement each game.
With thrills for your faithful supporters who came.
And the play of the year that stands out above all,
The day when young Adam took off with the ball.

A ninety-yard romp for a touchdown you say?
No a funny thing happened to him on the way.
When nearing the end zone with no one around,
His pants did him in—they began to fall down.

A major decision then had to be faced.
I'm sure you agree what he did showed good taste.
He opted for dignity, that above all.
He clutched at his pants, but surrendered the ball.

Well that is our season, our best I would say.
You boys and your coaches helped make it that way.
There isn't a doubt—you are all number one.
And thank you for showing that football is fun.

circa 1978

THE GREEN AND THE GOLD
THE RED AND THE BLUE

St. Patrick's and autumn means football is near
With tryouts at Finley to start the new year.
The coaches assembled that mid-August day
To try and decide just how well you could play.

To make each new team soon a draft would take place
The problem as coach—put a name with each face.
Who's that in the shorts and the purple tank top?
Throwing passes like Namath even I couldn't drop.

And that blonde headed guy—there's no doubt he can run
If he's still around, let's pick him number one.
Yes, the coaches were busy that first week or two
Taking copious notes on what player was who.

The teams were selected—each boy had a place
The Red team's new coach had a smile on his face.
The Green coaches whispered, "The best kids are ours."
While the Blue and the Gold said, "We picked only stars."

Then came opening day—not sunny nor dry
And the Green and the Gold played a great scoreless tie.
The Devils ran counters for win number one.
The Colts scored a touchdown—an eighty-yard run.

Excitement continued each week after week.
We hardly had noticed the Gold Rushers streak.
In five games they played, they were winners in four.
But more to the point, no opponent could score.

The Colts took them on in a wonderful game.
Both teams on defense, they were almost the same.
A shutout again—not a touchdown put in.
The tie for the Colts just the same as a win.

Their next anxious moment—the Devils late drive.
With seconds remaining, first down from the five.
The Red moved it closer—now inches to go.
The last play a touchdown? The ref, he said "No!"

And that is what happened this year at St. Pats.
The Gold finished first, we all tip them our hats.
They surely are good. Why? Stop and think what this means.
They got there by beating three very good teams.

So a toast to you all. To your coaches "Well Done"
It is you who have made this a season of fun.
And to all who support us. Most thanks go to you
From the Gold and the Green—The Red and the Blue!

circa 1982

*It is all up to the coach to keep fun
in the games our young children play!*

AFTERWORD

Keeping sports fun for kids is the overriding theme of this book and there are specific suggestions on how to accomplish this in the various chapters. Perhaps, though, some coaches or parents may still be wondering exactly what I mean when I say, "Keep sports fun for kids."

In response, let me summarize what I think is "fun for kids." It is not very different from what is fun for anyone. Fun is doing something you enjoy. Fun is feeling good about yourself. Fun is participating. Fun is doing things, hearing things or seeing things that make you and others laugh. Fun means belonging, not being rejected; being praised, not ridiculed; being congratulated, not criticized; succeeding, not failing. Fun is being appreciated or recognized by parents, friends, peers or just about anybody.

Things that are new or exciting can be fun. Pleasant surprises are fun. Accomplishments are fun, and so is trying. Satisfaction is fun. Competing is fun. Expressing yourself is fun. Contributing is fun and, of course, winning can be fun.

It occurred to me, while considering the meaning of fun, that perhaps my opinion was not the one that mattered. What kids think is fun is what really counts, so here are a few responses from a group of boys and girls between the ages of 7 and 11 who were questioned about what fun means to them:
- "playing and being happy"
- "having a race with your friends, even if you don't win"
- "having a good time"

- "feeling good about how you play"
- "thinking about making a good play even though you're just pretending"
- "being a good sport"
- "hitting a home run or catching the ball"
- "doing something that makes me feel good"
- "being with your friends"
- "trying and getting better"
- "it's just a game, and all that matters is having fun"
- "winning is fun but I still have fun even if we lose"
- "playing right field isn't much fun"
- "not getting a chance to play isn't fun"
- "sometimes it's not fun for the kids that aren't very good. They don't play much because the coach wants to win the game."
- "some kids don't have fun, but their parents make them play anyway"
- "cheating isn't fun"
- "it's not fun when my coach yells at me"
- "it's not fun if the game is canceled"

Without exception, every child questioned would rather play on a losing team than sit on the bench for a winning team. Most felt that winning wasn't as important as having fun, and that it wasn't necessary to win to have fun.

Given these responses, it should be clear where the emphasis should be and what needs to be done to "Keep sports fun for kids."

APPENDIX A

National Alliance for Youth Sports
National Standards for Youth Sports

Standard #1 Proper Sports Environment

Parents must consider and carefully choose the proper environment for their child, including the appropriate age and development for participation, the type of sport, the rules of the sport, the age range of the participants and the proper level of physical and emotional stress.

Background: There is a wide variety of youth sports experiences available to children. Some of these begin as early as 5 years of age and include both collision and non-collision sports, elite and recreational play categories, single-age and multi-age participation ranges and instructional to highly organized and competitive programs.

Rationale: Because all children physically and emotionally mature at different rates, parents must evaluate very carefully their child's youth sport experience.

Implementation:

1. Leagues will establish a minimum play rule per game for all children regardless of ability. (EVERYONE PLAYS RULE)

2. Leagues will organize programs within a 2 year range such as 5-6, 7-8, 9-10, 11-12, etc.

3. Leagues will allow post-season play only for regular season teams and not engage in choosing post-season All-Star teams. (NO ALL-STARS)

4. Leagues will establish a policy for not cutting players and will provide an opportunity for meaningful play for all children.

5. If awards are given, leagues will give participation awards and reduce emphasis on competitive trophies. (EVERYONE GETS AN AWARD)

6. League standings will not be used below the age of 9 and will be de-emphasized below the age of 13 by using techniques such as publishing only end-of-season results.

Standard #2 Programs Based on the Well-Being of Children

Parents must select youth sports programs that are developed and organized to enhance the emotional, physical, social and educational well-being of children.

Background: Many organized play experiences for children are carbon copies of adult-oriented programs. The rules, skill expectations and competitive requirements are the same as in high school, college and professional levels.

Rationale: Youth sports programs should be based on maximum participation. The program should focus on organizing meaningful play. Coaches should let children be involved in making decisions. The level and length of athletic competition should be commensurate with the physical and emotional development of the child.

Implementation:

1. Leagues will organize programs using the following guidelines:

A. 5-to 6-Year Old's-Developmental Program
-no regular competitive teams
-scores and/or standings not kept
-rules, equipment and field modified
-limit uniforms to T-shirt and hat
-no scheduled leagues, tournaments or All-Star competition
-leagues and coaches not permitted to require sports specialization
-co-rec play
-no travel
-coaches permitted on playing surface

B. 7- to 8-Year Old's-Sports Introduction Program
-informal teams
-scores and standings not kept
-rules, equipment and fields modified
-limited uniforms
-no tournament, post season play or All-Star competition
-co rec play encouraged
-travel within local community only
-coaches permitted on playing surface
-leagues and coaches not permitted to require sports specialization

C. 9- 10-Year Old's-Organizational Program
-scores kept but standings de-emphasized
-rules, equipment, and fields modified where necessary
-no out-of-community post-season play
-no national tournamment participation

-leagues and coaches not permitted to require sports specialization

   D. 11-to 12-Year Old's-Skill Enhancement Program
   -reasonable uniform policy
   -limited ability grouping used with proper grouping procedures
   -encourage a variety of position and situational play

2. Coaches will be required not to teach the use of sports to punish opponents through physical contact or excessive score domination.

3. Year-round participation must not be required by league or coaches.

4. Leagues must adopt rules banning rapid weight loss/gain procedures used solely for participation in youth sports.

5. Children below the age of 11 should participate in activities that contain limited collision potential and feature modified rules that will significantly reduce the chance of injury.

6. Leagues must consider weight and skill in grouping children.

7. Coaches must apply proper principles of conditioning and nutrition.

Standard #3 Drug, Tobacco and Alcohol-Free Environment

Parents must encourage a drug, tobacco and alcohol-free environment for their children.

Background: Pressures and opportunities for children to be involved in drug, tobacco and alcohol abuse have increased to crisis proportions during the past decades. Unsupervised social interaction and unknowledgeable adult leadership have contributed to the problem.

Rationale: Coaches and parents must be educated about all drugs, including performance enhancement chemicals. Leagues should have policies dealing with drug, tobacco, and steroid use and emphasizing prevention through education. Parents, league administrators, and coaches should be taught what to look for in abuse of these drugs and know how to access community resources for assistance on drug-related problems.

Implementation:

1. Leagues will adopt rules prohibiting the use of alcohol, illegal substances or tobacco by coaches, league administrators or game officials at all youth sports events.

2. Leagues will provide coaches and parents educational information on identifying signs and symptoms of substance use by children.

3. Leagues will establish policy and implementation procedures for immediately dealing with substance use by coaches and players and communicate these policies to coaches, players and parents.

4. Leagues will continually encourage dialogue between coaches, players and parents about the need for an alcohol, tobacco and drug-free environment for children.

Standard #4 Part of a Child's Life

Parents must recognize that youth sports are only a small part of a child's life.

Background: The foundation for human development occurs during the early years of life. Individuals are exposed to many different learning situations to increase their potential for successful development.

Rationale: Parents, coaches and league administrators need to encourage children to be involved in a variety of activities while recognizing the home, church, school and a variety of other social experiences are all a part of a child's growth and development. Parents must respect a child's decision not to play. Coaches and parents must realize that youth sports involvement also has ramifications for the entire family. Parents should insist that youth sports participation not detract from the child's academic progress.

Implementation:

1. Leagues will adopt a policy that allows for and encourages participation in a variety of youth activities in addition to the child's particular sport.

2. Leagues and coaches will not demand year-round involvement in a particular sport as a condition for meaningful participation.

3. Leagues will establish rules that limit organized practices to no more than 1 hour a day and 3 days a week through the age of 12 and not more than 1-1/2 hours and 4 days a week through the age of 16.

4. Leagues will adopt a policy that makes provisions for excused absences through parental requests for church, school and other family activities.

Standard #5 Training

Parents must insist that coaches be trained and certified.

Background: Sports participation can lead to harm if those responsible have no training. In most cases, youth sports organizations allow volunteers to coach without performing any background check.

Rationale: Parents should insist that coaches are educated in the following areas: psychological and emotional needs of children, safety and first aid, conditioning and nutrition, teaching proper sports techniques and drug awareness.

Implementation:

1. Leagues will require that coaches be annually trained and certified in the areas of the emotional needs of children, safety and first aid, conditioning and nutrition, teaching proper sports techniques and drug and tobacco education.

2. League administrators and officials must also be trained in the aforementioned areas.

3. Leagues must use appropriate and available screening techniques for selecting and assigning coaches to ensure that children are protected from abuse.

4. Leagues are encouraged to provide additional educational resources for coaches to assist them in providing the best possible youth sports experience for each child.

5. All coaches must sign a code of ethics pledging their commitment to provide an enjoyable, healthful youth sports experience.

Standard #6 Parents' Active Role

Parents must make a serious effort to take an active role in the youth sports experience of their child, providing positive support as a spectator, coach, league administrator and/or caring parent.

Background: Many parents pass their youngsters over to others, relying on someone else to take responsibility for their children's youth sport experience.

Rationale: Parents are key. They need to demonstrate the positive benefits of a youth sports experience by attending games, practices, or team social events; or by just expressing their positive support. Parents should discuss with their child why the child is participating and help him/her in evaluating his/her experience.

Implementation:

1. Parents will be required to attend a league orientation meeting. This may be one-on-one with the league official, if necessary.

2. Teams will be required to have a minimum of one team/parents' meeting each sports season.

3. Leagues will advertise parental involvement in roles such as coach, team manager, fund-raiser, league manager, special assistant and fan.

4. Leagues will encourage parent-child communication about their youth sports experience through newsletters, team meetings, coach-parent and coach-player discussions and league handbooks and guidelines.

Standard #7 Positive Role Models

Parents must be positive role models exhibiting sportsmanlike behavior at games, practices, and home while giving positive reinforcement to their child and support to their child's coaches.

Background: Children will follow the example of the adult role model and, in particular, the parent. Children will copy or imitate their parents' sports behavior, including the development of values based on that behavior.

Rationale: If the youth sports experience is to be a positive one for each child, parents must demonstrate sportsmanlike behavior as a fan, coach and league administrator. They need to encourage fun, give lots of praise for the little successes along the way and, when a child makes a mistake, separate the mistake from the child. Parents need to encourage peer support and give positive verbal support to team members, opponents and coaches of their child.

Implementation:

1. Leagues will develop a sportsmanship/conduct code including unacceptable behavior, e.g. berating players, coaches, officials; use of vulgar language; intoxication.

2. Leagues will communicate conduct requirements to coaches, parents, players and spectators through newsletters, handbooks, posting and announcements.

3. Leagues will develop an enforcement plan for implementing a sportsmanship code, including removal procedures.

Standard #8 Parental Commitment

Parents must demonstrate their commitment to their child's youth sports experience by annually signing a parental code of ethics.

Background: Individuals that sign commitments are usually more positive and supportive of their children.

Rationale: The parents should be knowledgeable of the opportunities and responsibilities for having their child involved in youth sports. They should also be requested to demonstrate their commitment by signing a code which outlines the opportunities their child should have through participation, as well as the responsibility the parent has in supporting the youth sports experience.

Implementation:

1. Participation will not be allowed for parents or guardians who refuse to sign the parental code of ethics.

Standard #9 Safe Playing Conditions

Parents must insist on safe-playing facilities, healthful playing situations and proper first aid applications, should the need arise.

Background: Children participating in youth sports are exposed to a variety of facilities, training programs and risk-taking opportunities. Most adult leaders do not have coaching degrees or a university coaching certificate.

Rationale: Coaches and league administrators have the responsibility to inspect and insure proper maintenance of facilities; have knowledge of proper equipment fitting, selection and appropriate use; understand the physical consequence of improper skill techniques; have the ability to modify rules for safe-playing situations; understand the physical need for a proper child-oriented conditioning program; understand proper weight control practices and have knowledge of prevention and first aid for athletic injuries, including the ability to implement emergency procedures.

Implementation:

1. Leagues will develop procedures for inspecting playing facilities for safety hazards before every youth sports activity.

2. Leagues will select equipment designed to insure injury reduction for participants (e.g. baseballs designed to reduce injuries, soccer shin guards, approved protective equipment in contact sports).

3. Leagues will be required to develop procedures for continual safety inspections of all playing equipment.

4. Leagues will ensure that teams have a fully equipped first aid kit at all youth sports activities.

5. Leagues will develop a plan for coaches on how to handle all emergencies at youth sports activities.

6. Leagues will establish procedures to ensure that all teams and events have an emergency first aid plan and equipment for dealing with injuries, hazards and weather conditions.

7. Leagues will not allow participation during unsafe conditions, such as lightning storms, darkness, playing sites in disrepair, etc.

8. Leagues will remove coaches that knowingly require or allow a player to play while having a serious injury or knowingly create unsafe play situations,

9. Leagues should require coaches to take CPR and advanced first aid training,

Standard #10 Equal Play Opportunity

Parents, coaches, and league administrators must provide equal sports play opportunity for all youth regardless of race, creed, sex, economic status or ability.

Background: The cost of participation in youth sports has risen dramatically during the past several years as have the number of single-parent families. Although sports opportunities for girls and racial minorities have improved, many adults still fail to recognize the contribution of the youth sports experience for all children.

Rationale: All children must have the opportunity to play regardless of race, creed, sex, economic status or ability. The coaches and league officials should recognize sex/role stereotyping and demand that racial prejudice of any type be prohibited. Every effort should be made to provide financial assistance to those youngsters unable to afford participation, including the cost of safe equipment. Adult youth sports leaders must teach a tolerance of, and respect for, people of abilities, sizes, shapes, colors, cultural and economic backgrounds. Youth sports should be a growth, rather than a limiting experience.

Implementation:

1. Leagues must adopt a non-discrimination policy that insures participation for all youngsters regardless of race, creed, sex, economic status or ability.

2. Leagues will make provisions so that all youngsters may be able to participate regardless of their financial ability to pay.

3. Leagues are encouraged to provide co-recreational programs through age 12.

4. Leagues will adopt an affirmative action coaching recruitment policy that will provide for recruitment and selection of qualified women and minorities.

Standard #11 Drug, Tobacco and Alcohol-Free Adults

Parents, coaches, fans and league administrators must be drug, tobacco and alcohol-free at youth sports activities.

Background: Sports participation has long been characterized as a means of developing character and positive values. Recent information indicates that competitive pressures, negative sports peer group associations and unhealthy adult role models may actually increase the risk of drug, tobacco and alcohol use among participants.

Rationale: Because of the influence they exert, parents involved in youth sports should understand that they must refrain from substance use, including smoking, alcohol consumption, chewing tobacco and illegal drugs at games, practices and other youth sports events. Healthful role modeling should lead the way in influencing youngsters to avoid drug, tobacco and alcohol use.

Implementation:

1. Leagues will require coaches, league administrators and game officials to refrain from the use of alcohol, illegal substances and tobacco at youth sports events

2. Leagues will require that alcohol not be sold or allowed to be brought into youth sports games and practices.

3. Leagues will encourage spectators not to use tobacco at youth sports events.

4 Leagues will develop an enforcement plan for removing coaches, parents and spectators who are under the influence of alcohol or illegal substances.

APPENDIX B

Parents' Association for Youth Sports
Parents' Code of Ethics

I hereby pledge to provide positive support, care, and encouragement for my child participating in youth sports by following the Parent's Code of Ethics:

• I will encourage good sportsmanship by demonstrating positive support for all players, coaches and officials at every game, practice or other youth sports event.

• I will place the emotional and physical well-being of my child ahead of my personal desire to win.

• I will insist that my child play in a safe and healthy environment.

• I will require that my child's coach be trained in the responsibilities of being a youth sports coach and that the coach upholds the Coaches' Code of Ethics.

• I will support coaches and officials working with my child, in order to encourage a positive and enjoyable experience for all.

• I will demand a sports environment for my child that is free from drugs, tobacco and alcohol and will refrain from their use at all youth sports events.

• I will remember that the game is for youth--not adults.

• I will do my very best to make youth sports fun for my child.

• I will ask my child to treat other players, coaches, fans and officials with respect regardless of race, sex, creed or ability.

• I will read the NYSCA National Standards For Youth Sports and do what I can to help all youth sports organizations implement and enforce them.

_____

Signature